职业技术・职业资格培训教材

企业人力资源管理师
职业技能鉴定辅导练习

三级
第3版

ENTERPRISE HUMAN
RESOURCE PROFESSIONAL

── 编审委员会 ──

主　　任　　张　岚　魏丽君
委　　员　　顾卫东　葛恒双　孙兴旺　张　伟　李　晔　刘汉成
执行委员　　李　晔　瞿伟洁　夏　莹　任余礼　李旭旦

── 编审人员 ──

主　　编　　李旭旦
编　　者　　钱建华　林志军　任中玥　严庆怡
主　　审　　任余礼

中国劳动社会保障出版社

图书在版编目（CIP）数据

企业人力资源管理师（三级）职业技能鉴定辅导练习/人力资源和社会保障部教材办公室等组织编写. -- 3版. -- 北京：中国劳动社会保障出版社，2018

1＋X职业技术·职业资格培训教材

ISBN 978-7-5167-3458-2

Ⅰ.①企… Ⅱ.①人… Ⅲ.①企业管理-人力资源管理-职业培训-习题集 Ⅳ.①F272.92-44

中国版本图书馆CIP数据核字(2018)第131464号

中国劳动社会保障出版社出版发行

（北京市惠新东街1号 邮政编码：100029）

＊

北京市艺辉印刷有限公司印刷装订 新华书店经销
787毫米×1040毫米 16开本 12.75印张 242千字
2018年7月第3版 2020年1月第3次印刷
定价：35.00元

读者服务部电话：(010) 64929211/84209101/64921644
营销中心电话：(010) 64962347
出版社网址：http://www.class.com.cn

版权专有 侵权必究

如有印装差错，请与本社联系调换：(010) 81211666

我社将与版权执法机关配合，大力打击盗印、销售和使用盗版图书活动，敬请广大读者协助举报，经查实将给予举报者奖励。

举报电话：(010) 64954652

内 容 简 介

本辅导练习由人力资源和社会保障部教材办公室、中国就业培训技术指导中心上海分中心、上海市职业技能鉴定中心依据上海1＋X企业人力资源管理师（三级）职业技能鉴定细目组织编写，是《1＋X职业技术·职业资格培训教材——企业人力资源管理师（三级）第2版》（以下简称"教材"）的配套用书，为读者学习教材核心内容，检验所学知识和技能提供有益的帮助。

本辅导练习按单元进行编写，每一单元与教材中的各个篇相对应，提供有针对性的辅导练习题。辅导练习题配有答案，便于读者检验和巩固所学的内容。为方便读者熟悉企业人力资源管理师（三级）的鉴定考核形式，本辅导练习最后提供了企业人力资源管理师（三级）鉴定方案，并提供了相应的模拟试卷、参考答案及评分细则，以便读者对自己学习、掌握知识和技能的总体情况有一个正确的认识。

本辅导练习可作为企业人力资源管理师（三级）职业技能培训与鉴定考核的辅导练习用书，也可供全国中高等职业院校相关专业学生，以及相关从业人员参加三级企业人力资源管理师岗位培训、就业培训使用。

改版说明

《1+X职业技术·职业资格培训教材——助理人力资源管理师职业技能鉴定辅导练习》自2008年出版以来深受从业人员的欢迎，在企业人力资源管理师（三级）职业资格鉴定、职业技能培训和岗位培训中发挥了很大的作用。

2014—2015年，根据人力资源管理理论发展和国内实践的最新情况，以及人力资源政策法规的变化，人力资源和社会保障部教材办公室、中国就业培训技术指导中心上海分中心、上海市职业技能鉴定中心分别重新组织编写了第2版教材和辅导练习。

近年来，随着社会的发展和经济形势的变化，人力资源管理的价值日益凸显，"人力资源是第一资源"这一概念已经深入人心，人力资源管理是企业发展战略得以实现的基础和保证。为了使学员更好地掌握重点，与时俱进，本次对第2版辅导练习进行修订。本次修订广泛听取了学员、培训师、管理师和业内专家的意见，在三个方面做了调整：一是适应2015年以来相关政策法规的变化，深入透彻地检验人力资源管理的理论与实践；二是调整、修订并增加了部分技能案例题和模拟题，推动人力资源管理理论和实践的结合，更突出重点；三是专业英语部分内容更新了表述。

希望本辅导练习能更有效地帮助读者学习教材的核心内容，并且检验所学知识与技能的掌握程度。

前　言

　　职业培训制度的积极推进，尤其是职业资格证书制度的推行，为广大劳动者系统地学习相关职业的知识和技能，提高就业能力、工作能力和职业转换能力提供了可能，同时也为企业选择适应生产需要的合格劳动者提供了依据。

　　随着我国科学技术的飞速发展和产业结构的不断调整，各种新兴职业应运而生，传统职业中也愈来愈多、愈来愈快地融进了各种新知识、新技术和新工艺。因此，加快培养合格的、适应现代化建设要求的高技能人才就显得尤为迫切。近年来，上海市在加快高技能人才建设方面进行了有益的探索，积累了丰富而宝贵的经验。为优化人力资源结构，加快高技能人才队伍建设，上海市人力资源和社会保障局在提升职业标准、完善技能鉴定方面做了积极的探索和尝试，推出了1+X培训与鉴定模式。1+X中的1代表国家职业标准，X是为适应经济发展的需要，对职业的部分知识和技能要求进行的扩充和更新。随着经济发展和技术进步，X将不断被赋予新的内涵，不断得到深化和提升。

　　上海市1+X培训与鉴定模式，得到了国家人力资源和社会保障部的支持和肯定。为配合上海市开展的1+X培训与鉴定的需要，人力资源和社会保障部教材办公室、中国就业培训技术指导中心上海分中心、上海市职业技能鉴定中心联合组织有关方面的专家、技术人员共同编写了职业技术·职业资格培训教材。

　　职业技术·职业资格培训教材严格按照1+X鉴定考核细目进行编写，教材内容充分反映了当前从事职业活动所需要的核心知识与技能，较好地体现了适用性、先进性与前瞻性。聘请编写1+X鉴定考核细目的专家和相关行业的专家参与教材的编审工作，保证了教材内容的科学性及与鉴定考核细目、题库的紧密衔接。

　　职业技术·职业资格培训教材突出了适应职业技能培训的特色，使读者通过学习与培训，不仅有助于通过鉴定考核，而且能够有针对性地进行系统学习，真正掌握本职业的核心技术与操作技能，从而实现从懂得了什么到会做什么的飞跃。

职业技术·职业资格培训教材立足于国家职业标准，也可为全国其他省市开展新职业、新技术职业培训和鉴定考核，以及高技能人才培养提供借鉴或参考。

新教材的编写是一项探索性工作，由于时间紧迫，不足之处在所难免，欢迎各使用单位及个人对教材提出宝贵意见和建议，以便教材修订时补充更正。

人力资源和社会保障部教材办公室
中国就业培训技术指导中心上海分中心
上 海 市 职 业 技 能 鉴 定 中 心

目　　录

第一单元　人力资源规划
一、学习要求 …………………………………………………… 3
二、职业鉴定考核要点 ………………………………………… 3
三、练习题 ……………………………………………………… 4
四、参考答案 …………………………………………………… 14

第二单元　招聘与配置
一、学习要求 …………………………………………………… 19
二、职业鉴定考核要点 ………………………………………… 19
三、练习题 ……………………………………………………… 20
四、参考答案 …………………………………………………… 30

第三单元　培训与开发
一、学习要求 …………………………………………………… 37
二、职业鉴定考核要点 ………………………………………… 37
三、练习题 ……………………………………………………… 38
四、参考答案 …………………………………………………… 47

第四单元　绩效管理
一、学习要求 …………………………………………………… 53
二、职业鉴定考核要点 ………………………………………… 53
三、练习题 ……………………………………………………… 54
四、参考答案 …………………………………………………… 63

第五单元　薪酬福利管理
一、学习要求 …………………………………………………………………… 69
二、职业鉴定考核要点 ………………………………………………………… 69
三、练习题 ……………………………………………………………………… 70
四、参考答案 …………………………………………………………………… 80

第六单元　劳动关系管理
一、学习要求 …………………………………………………………………… 85
二、职业鉴定考核要点 ………………………………………………………… 85
三、练习题 ……………………………………………………………………… 86
四、参考答案 …………………………………………………………………… 95

第七单元　专业英语
一、学习要求 …………………………………………………………………… 101
二、练习题 ……………………………………………………………………… 101
三、参考答案 …………………………………………………………………… 160

企业人力资源管理师（三级）鉴定方案 …………………………………………… 163
理论知识考试模拟试卷 …………………………………………………………… 164
理论知识考试模拟试卷参考答案 ………………………………………………… 178
专业技能模拟试卷 ………………………………………………………………… 179
专业技能模拟试卷参考答案 ……………………………………………………… 182
专业英语模拟试卷 ………………………………………………………………… 185
专业英语模拟试卷参考答案 ……………………………………………………… 191

第一单元

人力资源规划

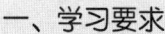

人力资源规划

一、学习要求

通过本单元的学习,学员应了解和掌握人力资源规划的相关知识与技能。本单元重点介绍人力资源信息分析、人力资源需求预测与供给预测的基本方法和流程;人力资源管理制度的基本要求和建设的主要步骤;工作设计的内容与方法、工作分析的流程和工作说明书编写的方法与技能等。

二、职业鉴定考核要点

1. 理论知识部分

鉴定范围	鉴定点	知识点	重要程度
人力资源预测	人力资源信息分析	人力资源信息	5
		人力资源信息的分析过程	
		人力资源信息的审核	
		人力资源信息的分析方法	
		人力资源信息分析报告的撰写	
	人力资源需求预测	人力资源需求预测的影响因素	5
		人力资源需求预测方法	
		人力资源需求预测步骤	
	人力资源供给预测	人力资源供给的影响因素	5
		人力资源供给预测方法	
		人力资源供给预测步骤	
	人力资源供求平衡	人力资源供求平衡的影响因素	5
		人力资源供求动态平衡	
人力资源管理制度及其建设	人力资源管理制度概述	人力资源管理制度的构成	5
		人力资源管理制度的特征	
		人力资源管理制度的基本要求	
	人力资源管理制度建设	人力资源管理制度建设的原则	5
		人力资源管理制度建设的程序	
		人力资源管理制度建设的步骤	
工作设计与工作分析	工作设计	工作设计的概念	9
		工作设计的原则	
		工作设计的内容	
		工作设计的方法	
		岗位设置的形式	

续表

鉴定范围	鉴定点	知识点	重要程度
工作设计与工作分析	工作分析	工作分析的主体	9
		工作分析的流程	
	工作说明书编制	工作描述	9
		工作规范	
		工作说明书的编制要求	
		工作说明书的内容安排	

2. 技能部分

序号	鉴定内容	重要程度
1	人力资源信息分析	5
2	人力资源需求与供给预测	5
3	人力资源动态平衡	9
4	人力资源管理制度建设	5
5	工作分析流程管理	9
6	工作说明书编制	9

三、练习题

【理论知识部分】

● (一) 判断题 (下列判断正确的请打"√",错误的请打"×")

1. 人力资源规划的实质是促进企业实现其目标,具有战略性、前瞻性和及时性的特点。( )

2. 人力资源规划最显著的特点是把员工看作资源。( )

3. 企业员工年龄以呈金字塔形分布为宜。( )

4. 通过广泛的人力资源调查,可以得到大量的人力资源信息,这些人力资源信息应直接用于人力资源规划工作,以确保数据的真实性。( )

5. 通过对员工类别的分析,可了解一个企业业务的重心所在。( )

6. 员工素质分析就是分析现有工作人员的性格特征和心理素质。( )

7. 在人力资源信息处理的二次审核阶段,需要对整理好的人力资源信息再一次进行审核,并根据审核中发现的问题,再次补救或纠正。( )

8. 人力资源信息审核的完整性是指要检查信息内容是否合理、统计口径是否一致、计算是否准确、计量单位是否合适、前后是否一致等。( )

9. 在人力资源信息的审核中,如果发现计算错误导致数据偏差,要采取修正方法,通过对原始数据的再次计算进行更改。（   ）
10. 人力资源信息的处理,包括定性和定量两种方法。（   ）
11. 人力资源信息处理的定性方法通常包括统计分组法和综合法。（   ）
12. 人力资源信息分析资料是对企业相关人力资源信息分析的结果,一般以分析报告的形式面世,称为人力资源信息分析报告。（   ）
13. 人力资源需求预测是指根据企业的发展规划和企业的内外条件,选择适当的预测技术,对人力资源需求的数量、质量和结构进行预测。（   ）
14. 在人力资源需求预测时,还要掌握预测中的定性、定量、时间和数量四个基本要素。（   ）
15. 德尔菲法是把专家聚拢在一起集体讨论,做出预测。（   ）
16. 德尔菲法的专家可以是组织内部专家,也可以是外聘专家。（   ）
17. 在人力资源需求预测的方法中,定量预测方法的使用使管理部门直接参与到人才需求预测过程中,综合考虑技术变化、工作负荷变化、组织变化等;而定性方法提供了一种有效的补充信息。（   ）
18. 人力资源供给预测是人力资源规划中的核心内容,是预测在某一未来时期,外部劳动力市场所提供的一定数量、质量和结构的人员,以满足企业为达到目标而产生的人员需求。（   ）
19. 马尔可夫分析方法适用于企业政策不稳定或有较大变化的企业。（   ）
20. 对于管理人员供给的预测,最简单有效的方法就是制订管理人员接替计划。（   ）
21. 员工档案是预测人员供给的有效工具,它包含每个人员技能、能力、知识和经验方面的信息。（   ）
22. 合理规划、及时执行,可以实现企业人力资源供求平衡。（   ）
23. 发展职能由以下活动组成:有效激励员工,能够始终保持员工有效工作的积极性、主动性和创造性,使其潜质得以充分发挥;为员工提供安全、健康、舒适的工作环境和条件,营造良好的企业文化氛围。（   ）
24. "见人又见物"是以工作任务为中心的管理哲学。（   ）
25. 以任务为中心的管理哲学把员工视为社会人。（   ）
26. 以任务为中心的管理哲学着眼于企业的长期目标。（   ）
27. 以人为中心的管理哲学采取的管理方式是民主—尊敬—参与。（   ）
28. 国家法律法规明确说明"不应该做什么,不应该怎么做"时,企业千万不能去做;而没有说明"不应该做什么或不应该怎么做"时,企业也要谨慎地做。（   ）
29. 企业的人力资源管理体系是企业精神、经营理念、价值观念等意识形态的集中表现。（   ）

30. "见物不见人"的管理哲学认为员工是具有能动性的重要资源。（　）
31. 以任务为中心的管理哲学认为员工是人工成本的承担者。（　）
32. 以人为中心的管理哲学强调沟通、协调、合作。（　）
33. 以任务为中心的管理哲学使用物质刺激作为员工管理和激励的手段。（　）
34. 人力资源管理制度建设必须同时考虑实现企业战略目标的前提，以及员工期望目标和员工职业发展的实现，推动企业实现战略目标。（　）
35. 一项具体的人力资源管理制度由总则、主文和附则等内容组成。（　）
36. 工作设计把工作的内容、工作的资格条件和报酬结合起来，目的是满足员工和组织的需要。（　）
37. 工作设计对于激发员工的积极性、增强员工的满意感和提高工作绩效都有重大影响。（　）
38. 不相容职务分离的核心是内部牵制。（　）
39. 工作内容的设计是岗位设计的重点，一般包括工作广度、深度、宽度、工作的完整性和工作的反馈5个方面。（　）
40. 保证工作的深度能使员工有成就感。（　）
41. 组织分析法通常适用于大型企业的大范围重组项目。（　）
42. 工作设计方法中的标杆对照法适用于不太精确的项目范围。（　）
43. 基于团队的岗位设置应用范围不广，可在那些"项目型"的公司中应用。（　）
44. 基于能力的岗位设置，要求限制赋予直接管理者的责任。（　）
45. 基于任务的岗位设置是将明确的工作目标按照工作流程的特点层层分解到岗位。（　）
46. 基于任务的岗位设置在机器化大工业时代显得十分突出，其最大的缺点是只考虑任务的要求而忽视在岗者个人的特点。（　）
47. 工作分析指收集所有与职务相关的信息，以科学和系统的方法确定某职务的性质、职责、任务和要求，决定一项工作所应包含的工作项目及从事此项工作的必备知识、技术和能力，并提供与职务本身要求相关的其他信息。（　）
48. 工作分析可以以人力资源部为主导，也可以以用人部门为主导。（　）
49. 工作说明书的编制是对工作分析的结果加以整合从而形成具有企业规章效力的正式文本的过程。（　）
50. 工作描述又称岗位标准、任职资格，是指任职者要胜任该项工作必须具备的资格与条件。（　）

(二) 单项选择题（下列每题的选项中，只有1个是正确的，请将其代号填在括号中）

1. 人力资源信息的准确性、及时性和（　）决定了它的应用价值。
   A. 有效性　　　B. 可衡量性　　　C. 完整性　　　D. 可比性
2. 对人力资源信息的审核又称为复查，一般采用（　）的方式进行。

A. 专家评估　　　　　B. 抽样　　　　　C. 对比　　　　　D. 规划小组讨论

3. (　　) 不是影响人力资源需求的外部因素。

   A. 劳动力市场的变化　　　　　　B. 政府相关政策的变化

   C. 行业发展状况的变化　　　　　D. 企业目标的变化

4. (　　) 不是影响人力资源需求的内部因素。

   A. 企业目标的变化　　　　　　　B. 行业发展状况的变化

   C. 组织形式的变化　　　　　　　D. 企业最高领导层的理念

5. 相对而言，下面几种人力资源需求预测方法中，(　　) 最为简单。

   A. 工作负荷预测法　　　　　　　B. 德尔菲法

   C. 现状规划法　　　　　　　　　D. 分合性预测法

6. 企业要求下属各个部门、单位根据各自的生产任务、技术设备等变化的情况对本单位将来各种人员的需求进行综合预测，然后把下属各部门的预测数据进行综合平衡，从中预测出整个组织将来某一时期内各种人员的需求总数，是(　　)。

   A. 工作负荷预测法　　　　　　　B. 德尔菲法

   C. 现状规划法　　　　　　　　　D. 分合性预测法

7. 假定企业保持原有的生产技术不变，则企业的人力资源也应处于相对稳定状态，即企业各种人员的配备比例和人员的总数将完全能适应预测规划期内人力资源的需要，这种方法是(　　)。

   A. 工作负荷预测法　　　　　　　B. 德尔菲法

   C. 现状规划法　　　　　　　　　D. 分合性预测法

8. (　　) 的目标是通过综合专家们的意见来预测某一领域的发展，该方法是一种特别的专家意见咨询方法。

   A. 工作负荷预测法　　　　　　　B. 德尔菲法

   C. 现状规划法　　　　　　　　　D. 分合性预测法

9. 人力资源需求预测分为现实人力资源需求、未来人力资源需求和(　　)预测三部分。

   A. 现实人力资源供给　　　　　　B. 未来流失人力资源需求

   C. 现实人力资源流失　　　　　　D. 未来人力资源预算需求

10. 找出过去人事变动的规律，以此来推测未来人事变动趋势是企业内部人力资源供给预测方法中的(　　)。

    A. 现状规划法　　　　　　　　　B. 马尔可夫分析法

    C. 管理人员接替计划法　　　　　D. 未来人力资源供给预测法

11. 企业人力资源管理制度体系可以分为基础性管理制度和(　　)两个方面。

    A. 综合性管理制度　　　　　　　B. 员工管理制度

    C. 核心管理制度　　　　　　　　D. 生产经营管理制度

12. （　　）不属于基础性人力资源管理制度。
    A. 工作岗位分析与评价工作的规定　　B. 员工绩效管理规定
    C. 人员培训与开发的规定　　　　　　D. 工作时间规定
13. （　　）不属于员工管理制度。
    A. 人员培训与开发的规定　　　　　　B. 工作时间规定
    C. 女职工劳动保护与计划生育规定　　D. 员工奖惩规定
14. 奖惩、解聘等属于（　　）职能。
    A. 录用　　　　B. 保持　　　　C. 发展　　　　D. 调整
15. 企业经营活动中的授权、签发、核准、执行、记录等工作步骤必须由相对独立的人员或部门分别实施或执行，是工作分析中（　　）的要求。
    A. 专业分工原则　　　　　　　　　　B. 协调费用最小原则
    C. 不相容职务分离原则　　　　　　　D. 整合分原则
16. 对于工作量不足80%的岗位，及时进行撤岗、并岗，保证每一个岗位的负荷，使所有工作尽可能集中，并降低人工成本，是工作分析中（　　）的要求。
    A. 专业分工原则　　　　　　　　　　B. 协调费用最小原则
    C. 不相容职务分离原则　　　　　　　D. 整合分原则
17. 使员工认识到自己工作的重要性，工作的责任心增强，工作的热情提高，是（　　）要实现的目的。
    A. 工作广度　　B. 工作深度　　C. 工作自主性　　D. 工作的反馈
18. 即使是流水作业中的一个简单程序，也应是该程序的全过程，让员工见到自己的工作成果，感受到自己工作的意义，是保证（　　）的目的。
    A. 工作广度　　　　　　　　　　　　B. 工作深度
    C. 工作自主性　　　　　　　　　　　D. 工作完整性
19. 从整个组织的远景和使命出发，设计一个基本的组织模型，然后根据具体的业务流程需要，设计不同的岗位，属于工作设计方法中的（　　）。
    A. 组织分析法　　B. 关键使命法　　C. 流程优化法　　D. 标杆对照法
20. （　　）是适用于较小的项目范围的工作设计方法。
    A. 组织分析法　　B. 关键使命法　　C. 流程优化法　　D. 标杆对照法
21. （　　）不是工作分析小组的成员。
    A. 企业高层管理者　　　　　　　　　B. 工作分析人员
    C. 外部专家　　　　　　　　　　　　D. 职工代表
22. 制订工作分析的计划、审核和检查工作流程，是（　　）的职责。
    A. 人力资源部　　　　　　　　　　　B. 直线经理
    C. 公司高层领导　　　　　　　　　　D. 外部的专家和顾问
23. （　　）不是任职者在工作分析中的职责。

A. 参加数据收集 B. 参与工作分析面谈
C. 参与工作说明书草案的制定 D. 参与工作分析计划的制订

24. ( ) 不是人力资源部在工作分析中的职责。
A. 制订工作分析的计划 B. 对直线经理和任职者进行培训
C. 提供工作分析专业知识 D. 为执行工作分析的多方面工作授权

25. 工作描述的核心内容是任何一份工作描述都必须包含的部分，这些内容一旦缺失，就会导致人们无法对本工作与其他工作加以区分，包括工作标识、工作关系、工作职责、( )等。
A. 工作概要 B. 工作权限
C. 工作环境与工作条件 D. 工作负荷

(三) 多项选择题（下列每题的选项中，至少有2个是正确的，请将其代号填在括号中）

1. 人力资源信息非常丰富，常用的人力资源信息有（ ）等。
A. 人力资源数量 B. 员工类别 C. 员工素质
D. 年龄结构 E. 员工子女

2. 分析人力资源结构中主管职位与非主管职位，目的在于了解（ ）。
A. 管理人员的缺口 B. 组织中管理幅度的大小
C. 部门与层次的多少 D. 薪酬成本变化趋势
E. 主管是否胜任

3. 人力资源信息的处理过程可以分为原始人力资源信息的审核、（ ）等阶段。
A. 分类汇总 B. 形成信息资料 C. 综合分析
D. 验证 E. 调研

4. 由于各个企业的自身情况千差万别，在各种因素影响下，获取的人力资源信息就可能出现空白、偏差和失真。在各种补救措施中，修正、（ ）等技术应用得较为普遍。
A. 取舍 B. 补遗 C. 复原
D. 判定 E. 定性

5. 一份人力资源信息分析报告，主要包括（ ）等内容。
A. 所要分析的问题 B. 分析问题的过程
C. 分析问题的结论 D. 相应的对策措施
E. 中期战略规划

6. 人力资源需求的定量预测方法包括（ ）。
A. 分合性预测法 B. 回归分析法
C. 趋势外推法 D. 工作负荷预测法
E. 德尔菲法

7. 人力资源供给的外部影响因素包括（ ）等。

A. 社会生产规模的大小 B. 国家经济体制
C. 科学技术进步 D. 所有制结构
E. 未来离职/退休率

8. 技能档案包含每个人员技能、能力、知识和经验方面的信息，这些信息的来源包括（　　）。
A. 工作分析 B. 绩效评估
C. 员工简历 D. 教育和培训记录
E. 员工口述

9. 技能档案可用于（　　）等。
A. 人力资源规划　B. 人员的调动　C. 员工晋升
D. 解雇　　　　　E. 录用

10. 企业人力资源短缺的原因，也就是影响人力资源供求平衡的因素，主要包括（　　）等方面。
A. 业务高速发展 B. 培训与开发
C. 绩效管理 D. 员工流失
E. 当地文化

11. 当企业人力资源供大于求的时候，采用的常用办法包括（　　）等。
A. 辞退不合格员工 B. 合并和关闭某些机构
C. 加强培训工作 D. 减少员工工作时间
E. 提高招聘效率

12. 现代企业人力资源管理，是以组织中的人为对象的管理，在某种意义和程度上，它至少具有（　　）等基本职能。
A. 录用　　　B. 保持　　　C. 发展
D. 调整　　　E. 辞退

13. 人力资源规划主要由（　　）等构成。
A. 制度规划　B. 岗位规划　C. 组织规划
D. 费用规划　E. 战略规划

14. 人力资源管理制度的制定必须符合（　　）等基本要求。
A. 以企业具体情况为基本出发点 B. 能够满足企业的长远需要
C. 遵守法律和道德规范 D. 保持合理性和先进性
E. 以行业标准为范本

15. 员工管理制度包括（　　）。
A. 女职工劳动保护与计划生育规定 B. 员工奖惩规定
C. 员工绩效管理（目标管理）规定 D. 组织机构和设置调整规定
E. 员工薪酬等级划分标准

16. 基础性管理制度包括（   ）。
    A. 工作时间规定   B. 员工奖惩规定
    C. 员工绩效管理（目标管理）规定   D. 组织机构和设置调整规定
    E. 因公出差审批规定

17. 工作设计要遵循的原则包括（   ）。
    A. 专业分工原则   B. 协调效用最大原则
    C. 不相容职务分离原则   D. 整合分原则
    E. 定性定量结合原则

18. 工作设计的主要内容包括（   ）。
    A. 工作内容   B. 工作职责   C. 工作关系
    D. 工作指标   E. 工作场地

19. 工作职责设计主要包括（   ）等方面。
    A. 工作责任   B. 工作权力   C. 工作方法
    D. 工作关系   E. KPI（关键绩效指标）

20. 岗位设置的形式主要包括（   ）。
    A. 基于能力的岗位设置   B. 基于任务的岗位设置
    C. 基于团队的岗位设置   D. 基于战略的岗位设置
    E. 基于人员安置的岗位设置

21. 在工作分析中，组织高层管理者的工作内容包括（   ）。
    A. 提出工作分析的必要性，并在组织内发起工作分析的工作
    B. 为执行工作分析的多方面工作授权
    C. 在工作分析中进行协调
    D. 与涉及工作分析的员工沟通
    E. 制定组织战略规划，并按照战略规划进行工作分析

22. 在工作分析中，人力资源部的工作内容包括（   ）。
    A. 为实施计划建立时间框架
    B. 制订工作分析的计划、审核和检查工作流程
    C. 对直线经理和任职者进行培训
    D. 起到专业支持、服务和管理的职能
    E. 调研

23. 在工作分析中，直线经理的工作内容包括（   ）。
    A. 作为工作分析结果的验收者   B. 协助人力资源部实施工作分析计划
    C. 为工作分析提供相关的信息   D. 与涉及工作分析的员工沟通
    E. 制订工作分析计划、审核和检查工作流程

24. 工作分析小组的成员一般由（   ）组成。

A. 企业高层领导　　　　　B. 直线经理
C. 工作分析人员　　　　　D. 外部的专家和顾问
E. 职工代表

25. 工作描述指对组织中各类岗位（职位）的工作性质、（　　）等工作特性方面的信息加以规范和描述的文件。

A. 工作任务　　B. 工作能力　　C. 工作关系
D. 工作环境　　E. 工作报酬

【技能部分】

案例1

案例背景

海康公司是一家从事计算机软件开发的企业，经过十多年的拼搏努力，公司业务获得了快速发展，到 2015 年，各种产品的产量和销售额达到了一定的规模，公司经营也趋于稳定，并且拥有了一批高学历的计算机软件开发人才。公司的员工以年轻人为主，平均年龄为 30 岁。

公司坚守为客户提供最大化价值的服务理念，在业内形成了一定的品牌效应，并且制定了 3~5 年的业务增长目标。从 2016 年开始，公司业务逐步调整，产品更加丰富，客户服务更趋多元化。公司人力资源部在年初与总经理一起确定了当年公司人员编制和招聘计划。但在公司的经营过程中，时常有一些新的项目上马，尽管人力资源部积极做好新员工的招聘工作，依旧很难及时满足各部门对软件开发人员的需求，而且短时间内招聘来的新员工也难以发挥作用。同时，许多项目需要的人才既要有技术背景，又要有管理能力，这样的人才严重不足，影响了公司的正常业务发展。另外，人力资源部在年初也没考虑到会有 20%左右的软件开发人员流失，导致了一些项目的开展困难重重。

案例思考

1. 该公司在人力资源规划中存在什么问题？
2. 该公司进行人力资源需求预测时应该采取哪些步骤？

案例2

案例背景

阳江公司是一家从事家用电器生产与销售的股份制企业。由于业务起步较早，公司积累了不少忠实客户，连续多年销售高速增长，发展潜力被看好。

曾在外资企业工作的贺一平进入阳江公司工作，担任从综合部门独立出来的人力资源部的经理。贺一平上任后不久，就碰到了各式各样的管理问题。

新进入公司技术部的小王向人力资源部反映，招聘时说好是来做产品技术工作的，但技术部经理经常安排一些琐碎的事务性工作给他，导致他参与技术研发工作机会较少，很难发挥他的优势。而事务性的事情他不擅长，经常做得不到位。

财务部王经理到人力资源部要求招聘一名会计,贺一平对王经理说:"填写'招聘申请表',把岗位需求列出来,我马上安排人手给您物色人选。"王经理诧异地说:"'招聘申请表'是什么?我没有见过。"

于是,贺一平翻阅了公司现有的人力资源管理制度,发现公司现有的相关制度非常简单,是由另一家企业的管理制度改编而来的,甚至有些制度的文本页眉上还保留着那个公司的名称,而有些制度只有框架没有具体的实施细则,根本无法实施。

在薪酬方面,虽然公司业务快速发展,经济效益逐年提高,但员工薪酬基本保持不变,薪酬水平已经远远落后于竞争对手,严重影响了员工的积极性。各类人力资源管理制度中几乎没有促进员工成长和发展的内容,干部的提拔很多是凭领导喜好决定,随意性强,导致了一些骨干员工离职。

案例思考
1. 该公司在人力资源管理制度建设中违背了哪些原则?
2. 该公司应如何有效推进人力资源管理制度建设?

案例3

案例背景

赛录发展有限公司是一家高科技企业,随着公司业务的发展,人员不断增加。为了能够适应市场变化,公司的组织结构变动较频繁,导致很多岗位出现工作职责不清的情况。人力资源部经理将刘晓明叫到了办公室,交代他:"你是人力资源部唯一学管理的研究生,我决定由你负责对公司相关职位进行工作分析,明确每个职位的工作职责,要求一个月内完成这个任务。"

刘晓明有些为难,尽管自己是学管理的,但在人力资源管理专业方面缺乏系统训练,可领导布置的任务又不得不接受。于是,刘晓明先是查看了公司现有的工作说明书,该说明书是两年前编制的,确实存在不少问题:格式过于简单、内容不完整、职位描述不准确、有些工作内容已经不能适应当前的要求。于是,刘晓明不再依赖原有文件,开始竭尽所能地收集有关资料。首先,他进一步明确了现有的组织架构,搞清公司的定岗定编情况。然后,他利用网络,查询与每个职位有关的信息,并向人力资源部经理请教,依据自己对公司管理情况的理解进行取舍,完成了工作分析的资料收集工作,并在此基础上最终编制出各职位的工作说明书。

然而,当刘晓明把工作说明书下发到各部门作为管理依据时,各部门的经理和员工却不认可工作说明书表述的内容。

案例思考
1. 刘晓明在进行工作分析时存在什么问题?
2. 刘晓明应如何进行工作分析?

四、参考答案

【理论知识部分】

(一) 判断题

1. × 2. √ 3. √ 4. × 5. √ 6. × 7. √ 8. × 9. × 10. √ 11. × 12. √
13. √ 14. × 15. × 16. √ 17. × 18. × 19. × 20. √ 21. × 22. × 23. ×
24. × 25. × 26. × 27. √ 28. √ 29. √ 30. √ 31. √ 32. √ 33. √ 34. √
35. √ 36. √ 37. √ 38. √ 39. √ 40. √ 41. √ 42. √ 43. √ 44. √ 45. √
46. √ 47. √ 48. √ 49. √ 50. ×

(二) 单项选择题

1. C 2. B 3. D 4. B 5. C 6. D 7. C 8. B 9. B 10. B 11. B 12. D 13. A
14. D 15. C 16. B 17. C 18. D 19. A 20. C 21. D 22. A 23. D 24. D 25. A

(三) 多项选择题

1. ABCD 2. BC 3. ABC 4. ABC 5. ABCD 6. BCD 7. ABCD 8. ABD
9. ABCD 10. ABCD 11. ABCD 12. ABCD 13. ACD 14. ACD 15. AB 16. CD
17. ACD 18. ABC 19. ABC 20. ABC 21. ABC 22. BCD 23. BCD 24. ACD
25. ACD

【技能部分】

案例 1

答题思路

1. 该公司在人力资源规划中存在的问题

(1) 人力资源需求预测工作不全面。人力资源部和总经理在确定公司人力资源需求时缺乏对企业整体现状的盘点,未与各部门进行沟通,缺乏对各部门未来业务人员需求的了解。

(2) 人力资源供给预测缺失,未能充分考虑人员流失对未来人力资源需求的影响。

2. 该公司进行人力资源需求预测时应采取的步骤

(1) 进行现实人力资源的需求预测。应与相关部门经理沟通确定职务编制和人员配置,进行现有内部人力资源盘点,统计出人员的缺编、超编情况,以及是否符合职务资格要求,讨论确定当前的人员需求。

(2) 进行未来人力资源的需求预测。应根据企业发展规划和各部门业务目标确定工作量,再根据工作量的增长情况,确定各部门需增加的职务及人数,并进行汇总统计。

(3) 进行未来流失人力资源预测。目前,公司没有退休问题,可以根据各部门上一年度人员离职情况,对未来可能的离职人数进行预测。

(4) 将现实人力资源需求、未来人力资源需求和未来流失人力资源预测汇总,即可预测出公司人员的需求,以此为依据开展后续的人力资源招聘等一系列人力资源管理工作。

案例 2

答题思路

1. 该公司在人力资源管理制度建设中违背的原则

(1) 违背了"紧密结合企业实际情况"的原则。该公司的人力资源管理制度不是依据企业的实际情况制定的,而是直接套用了其他公司的制度。

(2) 违背了"促进企业与员工共同发展"的原则。该公司的制度重点关注的是企业的管理需求,没有促进企业与员工共同发展的内容。

(3) 违背了"根据企业的变化情况不断进行调整"的原则。该公司的薪酬管理等相关制度未能根据企业的发展适时调整以支持组织的发展。

2. 有效推进该公司人力资源管理制度建设的思路

(1) 编制人力资源管理制度草案。人力资源部应起草人力资源管理制度大纲,结合实际情况,注意适用性和表述措辞,完成人力资源管理制度草案编制。

(2) 广泛征求意见,认真组织讨论。该公司应通过建立相关工作小组广泛听取意见,对草案进行修订、完善,并通过合法程序,将相关人力资源管理制度交给工会或职工代表大会审批。

(3) 不断修改调整,充实完善。应在制度执行过程中总结经验教训,结合公司的发展进行及时的修订。

案例 3

答题思路

1. 刘晓明在工作分析时存在的问题

(1) 工作分析主体单一。工作分析仅由刘晓明一人主导,未能建立工作分析小组,缺乏公司高层领导、熟悉部门情况的人员和有工作分析经验的专业人员的参与。

(2) 信息采集方式不合理。刘晓明仅通过查询网上资料的方法和人力资源经理访谈法来收集工作有关信息,导致信息不全面。

(3) 工作分析完成后未进行审核确认。分析结束后,未与相关部门事先沟通、请其审核,导致结果依然存在偏差,未能有效解决岗位职责不明的问题。

2. 刘晓明应在明确工作分析流程的基础上,做好以下各阶段工作

(1) 准备阶段。重点要构建工作分析小组,通过内部的宣导,使相关人员(直线经理和员工)理解、配合并参与工作分析,并对实施人员进行专业培训。

(2) 调查阶段。在现有的基础上补充访谈,尤其是对直线经理和相关员工进行访谈。

(3) 分析阶段。对调研信息进行客观分析,形成有针对性的分析结果。

(4) 完成阶段。就形成的工作分析结果——工作说明书与各相关部门进行沟通,通过审核、修改,最终形成切实有效的工作分析成果。

第二单元

招聘与配置

招聘与配置

一、学习要求

通过本单元的学习，学员应了解和掌握人力资源招聘与配置的相关知识与技能。本单元重点介绍招聘计划的制订、招聘渠道的特点与操作、招聘广告的设计、招聘选拔的方法与流程、人员录用要求与步骤、人员配置和人员离职的各项原理及操作等内容。

二、职业鉴定考核要点

1. 理论知识部分

鉴定范围	鉴定点	知识点	重要程度
招聘计划与实施	招聘计划	招聘计划的制订过程	9
		招聘计划的内容与修订	
		招聘计划的审批与实施控制	
	招聘来源和渠道	内部招聘的概念和方法	5
		外部招聘的概念和方法	
	招聘广告	招聘广告设计的基本原则	5
		招聘广告的内容	
招聘选拔	知识测验	知识测验概述	5
		知识测验的优缺点	
		知识测验题的编制	
		知识测验的实施	
	心理测验	心理测验的特点	5
		心理测验对员工招聘的意义	
		招聘中的心理测验应用类型	
		招聘测评中的心理测验实施步骤	
	招聘面试	结构化面试	9
		面试流程的管理	
人员录用	人员录用概述	人员录用的原则	9
		人员录用的要求	
		人员录用的基本步骤	
	人员录用决策	人员录用的决策	5
		人员录用决策的方法	
	人员录用实施	人员录用通知	9
		办理入职手续	

19

续表

鉴定范围	鉴定点	知识点	重要程度
人员录用	人员录用实施	签订劳动合同	9
		进行新员工培训	
		试用期管理	
人员配置与离职管理	人员配置	人员配置的原则	5
		人员配置的匹配原理	
		人员配置的类型	
	离职管理	离职管理的概念	5
		离职原因分析	
		离职面谈	

2. 技能部分

序号	鉴定内容	重要程度
1	编制招聘计划	9
2	招聘广告分析与设计	9
3	知识测验组织	5
4	心理测验应用	5
5	面试过程管理	9
6	录用决策管理	5
7	新员工入职管理	9
8	离职面谈	5

三、练习题

【理论知识部分】

(一) 判断题（下列判断正确的请打"√"，错误的请打"×"）

1. 招聘计划是组织根据部门的发展要求，根据人力资源规划的人力净需求、工作说明的具体要求，对招聘的岗位、人员数量、时间限制等因素做出的详细计划。（   ）

2. 招聘计划应由人力资源部制订，然后由用人部门对它进行复核。（   ）

3. 招聘调研分析是为了判断未来变化对企业人力资源需求的影响。（   ）

4. 招聘计划制订以后，就要执行，不能修改。（   ）

5. 内部招募是指组织采用职位公告、岗位竞聘、部门推荐等方式在组织内部选出合适的人选到空缺岗位。（   ）

6. 一些调查结果显示，大部分管理职位都是由从组织内部提拔起来的人员来担任的。
（　）

7. 经过竞争、选拔、考核、甄选，安排最优秀的人选到空缺岗位上去，使其能充分发挥自己的特长，确保其能胜任该岗位工作，是内部招聘的合理配置，是用人所长原则。
（　）

8. 外部招聘是根据一定的标准和程序，从组织外部众多应聘者中选拔获取所需人选的方法。（　）

9. 在招聘中录用能力超出职位要求很多的优秀人才，可以为组织储备人才。（　）

10. 在实际招聘中，把自己的组织描述得非常好，来吸引更多的应聘者，是一种有效的手段。（　）

11. 招聘人员的形象、谈吐、待人接物等方面也很重要，因为这能反映出该组织成员素质的培养和人格的塑造，是外部招聘的一个重要环节。（　）

12. 网络广告可以覆盖全部人群，且成本低廉。（　）

13. 知识测验最明显的特点，就是以书面试卷或者口头表述的形式对应聘者进行提问，有效地测试应聘者在基础知识、专业知识、管理知识、相关知识、综合分析、文字表达等方面的情况。（　）

14. 心理测验主要是通过对人的一组可观测的样本行为进行有系统的测量，来推断人的心理特征的测评方法。（　）

15. 知识测验试卷不仅用来考察应聘者的知识和能力，同时还是组织形象和业务水平的体现。（　）

16. 知识测验无法考查应聘者的思想品德修养、工作态度、口头表达能力、灵活应变能力、组织管理能力、操作能力。（　）

17. 心理测验的客观性就是指测验能够客观地反映被测试者的心理状况。（　）

18. 人格测验主要包括态度、兴趣、动机、性格等的测验。（　）

19. 仪器人格测评是用科学的仪器对被试人格进行测试，以了解被试心理获得的一种科学测评方法。（　）

20. 投射测验注重人格的整体分析，而一般的人格测验往往只能测量某些人格特征。（　）

21. 一般能力测验，也是通常所说的智力测验。（　）

22. 一般能力测验，一般只能对个别被测试者进行测验。（　）

23. 特殊能力测验，也称为能力倾向测验，体现了经过适当训练或被置于适当环境下完成某种任务的可能性，即一个人能够获得新知识、新技能的一种潜能。（　）

24. 霍兰德的职业性向理论认为，每个人的性格和天赋决定了其职业性向，职业性向（包括价值观、动机、需要等）是决定一个人选择何种职业的重要因素。（　）

25. 结构化面试中，面试的内容在面试之前已经形成一个固定的框架（或问题清单），

主面试官根据框架对每个应聘者分别进行相同的提问。 （　）

26. 传统面试的一个突出问题是面试官的提问太随意，想问什么就问什么；同时评价也缺少客观依据，想怎么评就怎么评。 （　）

27. 结构化面试让应聘者和外界感受到组织招聘的公开、公正和公平。 （　）

28. 以工作分析为基础确定测评要素是结构化面试的重要特点。 （　）

29. 录用决策体现择优录用原则，就是广揽人才、选贤任能，在甄选结果的基础上为各个岗位选择最优秀的工作人员。 （　）

30. 决策主体是最后决定录用的人或机构，一般的原则是谁用人，谁拥有决定权，即"谁用人谁决策"。 （　）

31. 一般基层人员的录用，一般由用人部门主管或人力资源部主管单独决定即可。 （　）

32. 优秀的应聘者非常抢手，因此在确保决策质量的前提下，要尽快做出录用决策。 （　）

33. 组织的人才储备通常分为内储和外储两种，内储就是暂时把预留人才储存在组织内部。 （　）

34. 组织的人才储备通常分为内储和外储两种，外储就是要清楚组织需要的人才在哪里。 （　）

35. 员工录用是招聘的目的和成果。在招聘考核中选拔出来的合格人员，只有办理一定手续，才能成为组织员工。录用手续的办理是确定员工身份的依据。 （　）

36. 录用决策一旦做出，就应该立即通知被录用者。 （　）

37. 新员工培训的目的在于将新录用人员由社会人转变为组织人。 （　）

38. 劳动合同期限3个月以上不满1年的，试用期不得超过2个月。 （　）

39. 劳动合同期限1年以上不满3年的，试用期不得超过3个月。 （　）

40. 3年以上固定期限和无固定期限的劳动合同，试用期不得超过6个月。 （　）

41. 同一用人单位与同一劳动者只能约定一次试用期。 （　）

42. 人员配置是为了创造组织效能而进行的获取、使用和留任足够质量和数量劳动力队伍的过程。 （　）

43. 人员配置过程包括招募、选拔和雇用这几个关键的要素，同时还包含了人员流动过程中发生的步骤和活动。 （　）

44. 人岗匹配具体包括个人与岗位匹配、个人与团队匹配、团队与组织匹配。 （　）

45. 人员配置的主要类型有人员调配、人员晋升、人员流动。 （　）

46. 人员流动是指经主管部门决定而改变员工的职位或职务、工作单位或隶属关系的人事变动，包括在企业之间的变动和企业内部的变动。 （　）

47. 委任制是用人单位通过契约或合同形式聘任员工的一种任用制度。 （　）

48. 由董事会或者经理直接指定下属职位的任用制度，称为聘任制。 （　）

49. 员工离职的原因包括个人原因、组织内部原因和组织外部原因。　　　　(　　)

50. 离职面谈的目的在于从中发现与企业工作有关的信息或事情，以便雇主改进他们的工作。　　　　　　　　　　　　　　　　　　　　　　　　　　　　　　(　　)

(二) 单项选择题（下列每题的选项中，只有1个是正确的，请将其代号填在括号中）

1. 招聘调研分析主要调研两方面的内容，第一是根据本组织的发展与运行现状，明确工作任务及完成这些任务所需或所缺人员的情况，第二是（　　）。
   A. 分析本组织整体人力资源或者局部人力资源状况
   B. 分析本组织人力资源规划及当前的工作任务情况
   C. 确定招聘的范围、数量、规模等情况
   D. 确定如何开展招聘工作

2. 如果待招聘人员在人员预算范围外，需要（　　）对招聘的必要性进行审核和论证。
   A. 人力资源经理　　　　　　　　B. 部门经理
   C. 公司高层管理人员　　　　　　D. 用人部门

3. 一些调查结果显示，高达90%的管理职位都是由（　　）获得的。
   A. 外部招聘　　B. 内部招聘　　C. 猎头招聘　　D. 内部竞聘

4. 内部招募的信息覆盖面应是（　　）。
   A. 有关部门员工　　　　　　　　B. 整个组织内部的全体员工
   C. 后备人选库中的员工　　　　　D. 公司和部门领导推荐的人员

5. 无论是选拔优秀的员工到更高的职位上工作，还是通过考试将员工安排到更适合他的岗位上去，都应当让广大员工认识到，不断地提高自己的工作能力将会在组织内获得更大的发展空间，这体现了内部招聘的（　　）原则。
   A. 机会均等　　　　　　　　　　B. 任人唯贤、唯才是用
   C. 合理配置、用人所长　　　　　D. 激励

6. 当所招募的工作承担者较为专业，同时时间和地区限制不是最重要的时候，可以采用（　　）渠道发布招聘信息。
   A. 报纸　　B. 杂志　　C. 广播电视　　D. 网络

7. 招聘广告设计的AIDA原则（招聘广告形式原则）中，I是指（　　）。
   A. 能引起求职者的注意　　　　　B. 能激起求职者的兴趣
   C. 能激发人们求职的愿望　　　　D. 方便求职者的求职行为

8. 招聘广告设计的AIDA原则中，后面一个A是指（　　）。
   A. 能引起求职者的注意　　　　　B. 能激起求职者的兴趣
   C. 能激发人们求职的愿望　　　　D. 方便求职者的求职行为

9. 招聘广告的核心内容应包括两个方面，即职位所要求的胜任素质和（　　）。
   A. 企业优势展示　　　　　　　　B. 待遇福利条件

C. 告诉应聘者如何获得职位　　　　　D. 对符合要求的应聘者表示欢迎的态度

10. 招聘广告中，可以不提供的联系方式是（　　）。
    A. 公司地址　　　B. 电子邮件　　　C. 传真　　　D. 电话

11. 美国学者戈登（J. Gordon）、威尔逊（P. Wilson）和斯旺（H. Swan）在1982年通过对报纸读者的调查来了解企业招聘广告中各种信息的必要性，其中（　　）的必要性最高。
    A. 工作地点　　　B. 薪酬　　　C. 工作经历　　　D. 岗位职责

12. 下面关于知识测验表述错误的是（　　）。
    A. 采取书面试卷或者面试的形式　　B. 可以大规模进行
    C. 成本相对较低　　　　　　　　　D. 可能出现"高分低能"现象

13. 测验的题目、指导语、主试的言语和态度、测验实施时的物理环境等，均经过标准化，体现了心理测验的（　　）。
    A. 间接性　　　B. 相对性　　　C. 客观性　　　D. 可变性

14. 在对人的行为做比较时，没有一个绝对的零点，即没有绝对的标准，有的只是一个连续尺度上的行为序列。测量就是看每个人处在这个序列上的什么位置，这体现了心理测验的（　　）。
    A. 间接性　　　B. 相对性　　　C. 客观性　　　D. 可变性

15. 心理测验只能测量人的外显行为，即通过测量个体对测验题目的反应，推论其心理特质，体现了心理测验的（　　）。
    A. 间接性　　　B. 相对性　　　C. 客观性　　　D. 可变性

16. （　　）又称问卷法，即对拟测量的个性特征编制若干测试题（陈述句），被试者逐项给出书面答案，依据其答案来衡量评价某项个性特征。
    A. 自陈式量表法
    B. 投射测验
    C. 仪器人格测评
    D. MBTI（迈尔斯布里格斯类型指标）工作风格测验

17. （　　）基于如下假设：个体不是被动地接受外界的刺激，而是主动地、有选择地给外界刺激赋予某种意义，然后表现出适当的反应，人们可以从这些反应中推论他的人格。
    A. 自陈式量表法　　　　　　　B. 投射测验
    C. 仪器人格测评　　　　　　　D. MBTI工作风格测验

18. 下面关于投射测验的描述不正确的是（　　）。
    A. 呈现给被试者的是一个模糊而相对无结构的刺激情景
    B. 被试者知道测验的目的，因此反应具有针对性
    C. 被试者可以用各种方式来自由回答问题

D. 注重人格的整体分析

19. 霍兰德职业兴趣量表是一种应用广泛的（　　）量表。
    A. 人格测验　　　　　　　　B. 能力测验
    C. 职业适应性测验　　　　　D. 特殊能力测验

20. 职业适应性测验，有时也称为动力测验，它关注人对从事某项活动或职业的一种内在倾向，其理论基础是（　　）。
    A. 韦氏量表　　　　　　　　B. 霍兰德的职业性向理论
    C. MBTI工作风格测验　　　 D. 卡特尔人格因素测验

21. 在结构化面试中，面试官的人数必须在（　　）人以上。
    A. 2　　　　B. 3　　　　C. 4　　　　D. 5

22. 培训面试官是为了改变传统面试中面试官凭经验和直觉评价的问题，提高面试的准确性。面试培训一般包括理论知识培训和（　　）培训两大部分。
    A. 业务知识　　B. 实践技巧　　C. 公司文化　　D. 职业素养

23. 管理人员等关键岗位，一般由（　　）批准后录取。
    A. 部门经理　　　　　　　　B. 人力资源部经理
    C. 总经理　　　　　　　　　D. 人力资源部招聘经理

24. 在通知被录用者时，最重要的原则是（　　）。
    A. 合法　　　B. 及时　　　C. 有效　　　D. 全面

25. 离职面谈一般由（　　）进行。
    A. 人力资源部　　　　　　　B. 部门主管
    C. 公司总经理　　　　　　　D. 团队负责人

(三) 多项选择题（下列每题的选项中，至少有2个是正确的，请将其代号填在括号中）

1. 编制招聘计划的过程包括（　　）等步骤。
   A. 调研分析　　B. 预测　　C. 审核
   D. 决策　　　　E. 实施

2. 了解与分析本组织人力资源或者局部人力资源状况，内容主要包括（　　）等，目的是掌握组织人力资源现状和当前管理利用情况。
   A. 人员学历结构　　　　　　B. 技术结构
   C. 年龄结构　　　　　　　　D. 人力资源分布与分配状态
   E. 员工绩效构成

3. 对企业人力资源需求会产生影响的因素主要包括企业扩张、组织机构变化、（　　）等。
   A. 技术发展与革新　　　　　B. 竞争对手人才抢夺
   C. 劳动（工作）效率提升　　D. 劳动力市场的变化

E. 当地房价

4. 招聘决策是招聘计划的核心,具体包括招聘哪些岗位、需要多少人、（　　）等内容。

　　A. 招聘实施部门　　　　　　　　B. 招聘方法
　　C. 招聘测试的实施部门　　　　　D. 招聘预算
　　E. 招聘结束时间与新员工到位时间

5. 内部招募应遵循的基本原则包括（　　）。

　　A. 机会均等　　　　　　　　　　B. 任人唯贤,唯才是用
　　C. 合理配置,用人所长　　　　　D. 公开公平
　　E. 招之即来,来之能用

6. 内部招募的实施方法主要有（　　）。

　　A. 内部晋升或岗位轮换　　　　　B. 内部竞聘
　　C. 内部员工推荐　　　　　　　　D. 临时人员转正
　　E. 上级委派

7. 内部晋升或岗位轮换的前提条件是（　　）。

　　A. 组织有一套完善的职位体系
　　B. 要明确不同职位的关键职责、胜任素质、职位级别等晋升和岗位轮换中的运作依据
　　C. 要建立员工的职业生涯管理体系
　　D. 要有成熟的绩效管理体系
　　E. 要有充足的工资预算作为晋升后的保障

8. 外部招聘的主要方式包括（　　）。

　　A. 内部员工举荐　　B. 网络招聘　　　C. 猎头
　　D. 人才市场　　　　E. 临时人员转正

9. 外部招募应遵循（　　）等基本原则。

　　A. 公正公平原则　　　　　　　　B. 适用适合原则
　　C. 激励原则　　　　　　　　　　D. 沟通与服务原则
　　E. 合理配置,用人所长原则

10. 心理测验具有（　　）等特点。

　　A. 间接性　　　　　B. 相对性　　　　C. 主观性
　　D. 可变性　　　　　E. 可追溯性

11. 心理测验的标准化体现在（　　）等方面。

　　A. 题目确定的标准化　　　　　　B. 评分计分的方法经过了标准化
　　C. 分数的转换和解释经过了标准化　　D. 测试者的标准化
　　E. 测试场景的标准化

12. 心理测验对员工招聘的意义在于（   ）。
    A. 提高组织人才甄选的效度   B. 降低招聘成本，起到优胜劣汰的作用
    C. 提高招聘效率，实现批量测评   D. 可以直接为招聘确定录用人选
    E. 实施成本较低

13. 招聘中应用的心理测验类型主要包括（   ）。
    A. 人格测验   B. 智力测验
    C. 特殊能力测验   D. 职业适应性测验
    E. 品德测验

14. 能力通常包括（   ）。
    A. 一般能力   B. 动手能力   C. 特殊能力
    D. 思维能力   E. 行动能力

15. 一般能力是完成各种活动都必须具备的能力，主要包括（   ）。
    A. 注意力   B. 观察力   C. 记忆能力
    D. 数学能力   E. 决断能力

16. 特殊能力是从事某种活动所需要的能力，包括（   ）。
    A. 数学能力   B. 音乐能力   C. 绘画能力
    D. 思维能力   E. 观察能力

17. 招聘测评中的心理测验实施步骤包括通过工作分析定义什么是获得高绩效的能力要素及其结构体系、（   ）等。
    A. 选择测试方法 B. 实施测试   C. 交叉验证
    D. 运用结果   E. 通知求职者

18. 结构化面试一般由一系列连续向应聘者提出的与工作相关的问题构成，包括情景问题、（   ）等。
    A. 工作知识问题   B. 工作样本模拟问题
    C. 关键工作内容模拟问题   D. 个人经历
    E. 家庭背景

19. 结构化面试的结构化体现在（   ）。
    A. 面试全过程的结构化   B. 面试官的结构化
    C. 标准的结构化   D. 招聘流程的结构化
    E. 录用程序的结构化

20. 结构化面试的缺点主要包括（   ）。
    A. 不能充分发挥面试官的智慧、知识、经验和能力
    B. 不能给应聘者更大的展示才华的空间
    C. 缺少面试官与应聘者之间充分的双向沟通
    D. 不能根据应聘者的不同特点提出针对性的问题

E. 不适用于批量面试

21. 结构化面试比较适用于（　　）。

　　A. 大批量的面试　　　　　　　　B. 初步面试筛选
　　C. 中高级管理人员的招聘　　　　D. 普通员工的招聘
　　E. 专业技术人员的招聘

22. 完整的面试官团队应包括（　　）等，在确保基本面试官团队的基础上可在不同面试阶段有不同组合。

　　A. 人力资源经理　　B. 直线经理　　　C. 外部专家
　　D. 高层领导　　　　E. 同岗位员工

23. 人员录用必须遵循的原则包括（　　）。

　　A. 录用流程体现公平竞争的原则　　B. 录用决策体现择优录用的原则
　　C. 员工安置体现人岗匹配的原则　　D. 劳动关系符合法律的原则
　　E. 薪酬水平体现市场竞争力的原则

24. 通知应聘者是录用工作的一个重要部分，通知类型包括（　　）。

　　A. 录用通知　　　B. 辞谢通知　　　C. 聘任协议
　　D. 报到通知　　　E. 签订劳动合同的通知

25. （　　）不得约定试用期。

　　A. 以完成一定工作任务为期限的劳动合同
　　B. 劳动合同期限不满 3 个月的
　　C. 劳动合同期限不满 6 个月的
　　D. 稀缺人才
　　E. 劳动派遣员工

【技能部分】

案例 1

案例背景

　　启迪英语培训学校是一家具备培训资质的民营教育机构，随着市场需求的不断增长，学校业务发展非常迅速。为了进一步拓展市场，学校需要招聘 20 名市场专员。

　　为此，人力资源部对该岗位应聘者提出要求，市场专员的学历必须要大专以上。由于需对各类培训学校、其他市场及客户相关信息进行分析和处理，还要到学校周边独立开展市场咨询活动，吸引更多客户咨询培训学校的英语培训课程，进行学前英语培训推广，为学校招生创造有利条件，因此市场专员需要 2 年以上相关工作经验，要具有开展营销活动的能力。员工入职后，每月收入包括底薪和咨询量奖，学校每月为员工缴纳"五险一金"，享有国家规定的年休假。

　　培训学校希望能在 11 月 20 日前确定候选人，培训学校招聘的电子邮箱为：zhaopin@qidi.cn。

案例思考

请你为启迪英语培训学校撰写一份市场专员的招聘广告。

案例 2

案例背景

陆浩是精工公司负责产品设计与开发的工程师，准备下周与委托开发该项目的负责人洽谈合作内容。然而，陆浩收到人力资源部招聘主管通知，请他参与技术开发高级工程师招聘面试。这个职位要求应聘者有 7 年以上的工作经验。通常这类面试都是由技术开发部经理参加的，这两天经理出差，人力资源部听说陆浩在技术方面还是不错的，于是临时邀请陆浩代替经理参与本次招聘面试工作。

陆浩 3 年前通过校园招聘进入公司，对于招聘面试事前毫无经验，从没有担任过面试官。来到面试现场后，陆浩紧张地翻阅着手中的面试打分表和应试人员的自荐资料，但是面试打分表只列举了简单的指标，包括职位匹配度、人际沟通能力、专业技术能力、团队管理能力、创新能力等，并没有具体的打分标准。对于如何打分，陆浩心里完全没底。在人力资源部的提醒与催促下，陆浩只能凭感觉对应聘者过去的技术经历做了一些提问与记录。很快，6 名应聘者的面试结束了，陆浩也凭着自己的理解完成了打分。

案例思考

1. 请分析精工公司在本次招聘面试中存在什么问题？
2. 如果你是人力资源部主管，将如何改进面试准备工作？

案例 3

案例背景

新城公司是一家从事网络维修和信息服务的公司，成立至今已有 3 年。2017 年 6 月 1 日，王曦去新城公司应聘行政主管一职，经过 2 轮面试后公司告诉她回去等消息。2017 年 6 月 8 日，新城公司在对 5 位候选人进行面试后，决定录用王曦。人力资源部经理让招聘专员小李立即通知王曦。由于行政管理部门一直催促要人，小李电话通知王曦近期带好相关证件办理入职手续，并尽快来上班。6 月 10 日，王曦就向原单位递交了辞职报告，等待办理离职手续。

为确保新单位是自己满意的正规公司，王曦在 6 月 10 日也通过电子邮件询问招聘专员小李入职所需的材料，并希望收到正式的录用通知。由于小李近期工作较多，只是用短信告诉王曦只要原单位的材料及一些证件即可，希望她尽快来公司。

6 月 20 日，王曦在原单位办理好离职手续，立即来到新城公司人力资源部，但由于缺少体检报告、银行账户不对等原因没有成功办理入职手续。

一周后，王曦再到新城公司办理入职，由于缺少相关工作证明和社会保险转接账号，又没有顺利办好。直到 2016 年 6 月 28 日，公司才给她发送了录用邮件和录用所需资料清单。对此，招聘专员小李表示歉意，并同意王曦可以边上班边办理。由于公司月底发工资，而王曦还没有办好手续，故没有6月份一部分工资。王曦很失望地表示，公司办理入职程序不正规，导致她没有获得应得的工资。

案例思考

1. 新城公司在人员录用工作过程中存在哪些问题？
2. 请为新城公司编制一份员工入职流程。

案例4

案例背景

海森公司是一家中型股份制企业，是化学高分子材料制造行业中的领头羊。近5年来，公司产品销售收入以每年20%的速度递增。然而，今年以来公司的产品销售收入却并不理想。公司对产品进行的市场调研显示，老产品所占据的市场份额已经到了顶峰，某些产品销售量甚至开始下滑，直至6月份仅完成计划销售收入的35%。与此同时，人力资源部接到了不少员工的辞职申请，大部分是研发和销售人员。员工离职已经开始影响公司的业务了。

为此，人力资源部决定进行离职面谈，并由人力资源部经理、薪酬主管和相关部门经理组成面谈小组，在公司会议室与近期要求离职的15名员工开展了每人15分钟的谈话。在离职面谈过程中，由相关部门经理向每个员工了解离职原因，提出的问题主要有两个："为什么要离职？""以后有什么打算？"15名员工几乎异口同声是由于个人家庭等原因，本人对公司还是十分有感情的。人力资源部主管总感觉这些员工没有真实表达自己离职的真实原因，对相关部门经理的提问也有所顾忌。而这些部门经理对大家的离职也没有太多挽留的意思，面谈后希望人力资源部尽早找到替代者。

不久之后，业内开始流传该公司对人才不重视、管理混乱等负面评价，有不少新的候选人在听到这些消息后就不再应聘该公司的岗位了。

案例思考

1. 该公司在离职面谈中存在什么问题？
2. 该公司该如何有效组织离职面谈？

四、参考答案

【理论知识部分】

（一）判断题

1. √　2. ×　3. ×　4. ×　5. √　6. √　7. ×　8. √　9. ×　10. ×　11. √　12. ×　13. ×　14. √　15. √　16. √　17. ×　18. √　19. √　20. √　21. √　22. ×　23. √　24. √　25. √　26. √　27. √　28. √　29. ×　30. √　31. √　32. √　33. √　34. √

35. √ 36. √ 37. × 38. × 39. × 40. √ 41. √ 42. √ 43. √ 44. × 45. ×
46. × 47. × 48. × 49. √ 50. √

(二) 单项选择题

1. A 2. C 3. B 4. B 5. D 6. B 7. B 8. D 9. D 10. D 11. A 12. A 13. C
14. B 15. A 16. A 17. B 18. B 19. C 20. B 21. A 22. B 23. C 24. B 25. A

(三) 多项选择题

1. ABD 2. ABCD 3. ACD 4. BCDE 5. ABC 6. ABCD 7. ABCD 8. BCD
9. ABD 10. AB 11. ABC 12. ABC 13. ABCD 14. AC 15. ABC 16. ABC 17. ABC
18. ABC 19. ABC 20. ABCD 21. AB 22. ABCD 23. ABCD 24. AB 25. AB

【技能部分】

案例1

答题思路

招 聘 启 事

启迪英语培训学校是一家有培训资质的民营教育机构,因业务发展需要招聘若干名市场专员。

1. 岗位职责

(1) 负责调查与分析培训学校周边的相关市场信息。

(2) 策划并组织实施培训学校的推广活动。

(3) 吸引客户咨询,为学校招生创造有利条件。

(4) 完成领导安排的其他任务。

2. 任职要求

(1) 大专以上学历,2年以上市场营销相关工作经验。

(2) 沟通表达能力强,有临场应变能力。

(3) 有调查研究和数据分析能力。

(4) 能够独立开展市场活动。

3. 员工待遇

(1) 每月收入＝固定底薪＋咨询量奖。

(2) 所有员工入职后都按照规定的比例每月缴纳"五险一金"。

4. 申请资料与联系方式

有意者请在11月20日前将简历发至邮箱 zhaopin@qidi.cn。

案例2

答题思路

1. 公司在招聘面试中存在的问题

(1) 面试准备阶段准备不充分。面试官是临时调任的,未设计面试提纲与试题,面试评价指标不明确，缺乏具体的标准，容易导致评分的误差。

（2）面试实施阶段流程较简单。

（3）面试评价阶段比较草率。

2. 对面试工作的改进建议

（1）面试准备阶段。组建面试官团队，培训面试官，设计面试提纲与试题，拟定面试评价表，安排面试场地，准备面试资料与道具。

（2）面试实施阶段。正式的面试应包含关系建立阶段、导入阶段、正题阶段、深入阶段、面试结束阶段。

（3）面试评价阶段。面试结束后，考官应回顾面试记录，根据面试记录中的信息在面试评价表中对应聘者进行评价。

案例3

答题思路

1. 该公司在人员录用工作中存在的问题

（1）录用通知不规范、不及时。公司做出录用决定后仅通过电话和短信通知应聘者。

（2）人员录用流程不完善。没有及时通过正式的电子和书面文件通知应聘者携带办理入职手续所需要的资料等信息。

2. 员工入职流程

（1）人力资源部同意录用员工，发出人员录用通知书。

（2）录用员工与原单位解除劳动关系，离职后到公司办理入职手续。

（3）录用员工要到公司指定医院进行体检，体检合格员工按约定的时间正式入职。

（4）新员工到公司报到、填写登记表、签订劳动合同、办理工资卡、领取出入证件等。

（5）参加新员工入职培训。

案例4

答题思路

1. 该公司离职面谈中存在的问题

（1）离职面谈目的不明确，不是以挽留离职者为目的，使离职者有所顾虑，不愿透露太多的信息。

（2）离职面谈的流程不合理。缺乏面谈方案的准备，参加面谈人员过多，离职信息处理不全面，未对谈话资料进行保存。

2. 有效组织离职面谈的方法

（1）准备面谈方案。确定面谈目标、内容、方式、处理意见等。有意识降低离职对其他员工的负面影响和对企业形象的不利影响，明确发现问题寻求解决对策的定位，并做好

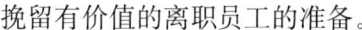

挽留有价值的离职员工的准备。

（2）和员工面谈沟通并了解相关信息。了解离职人员离职的真实原因、对公司当前管理文化的评价、对所在部门或公司层面的改进建议。离职面谈中要平等交流和沟通，注意倾听，做好记录。

（3）处理离职信息，做出处理决定。进行书面总结，分析离职原因，找出问题根源，研究改进方法，保存谈话资料并定期整理。将离职面谈报告按照规范的格式进行整理并分类保管。

3

第三单元

培训与开发

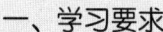

培训与开发

一、学习要求

通过本单元的学习,学员应了解和掌握人力资源培训与开发的相关知识与技能。本单元重点介绍培训需求分析的方法和步骤,培训计划的制订,培训方法、培训师、培训机构选择的方法和注意事项等。

二、职业鉴定考核要点

1. 理论知识部分

鉴定范围	鉴定点	知识点	重要程度
培训需求分析	培训需求分析概述	培训需求分析的概念	5
		培训需求分析的作用	
		培训需求分析的层面	
		培训需求分析的时机	
		培训需求分析中的常见误区	
	培训需求分析实施	培训需求分析的准备	5
		培训需求的调查	
		培训需求的确认	
		培训需求分析报告的撰写	
培训计划制订	培训目标设计	培训目标及其构成要素	5
		确定培训目标的意义	
		培训目标的确定	
	培训计划的编制	培训计划的含义	5
		培训计划的分类	
		培训计划的内容	
		培训计划的制订程序	
培训的组织实施	培训方法的比较与选择	培训方法的比较	9
		培训方法的选择	
	培训师的选用	培训师的要求	5
		培训师的类型	
		培训师的选择	
		培训师的培训	
	培训机构的选择	培训机构的选择步骤	5
		选择培训机构需要注意的问题	

续表

鉴定范围	鉴定点	知识点	重要程度
培训的组织实施	培训预算的编制	培训预算的构成	5
		培训预算的原则	
		培训预算的流程	
		培训预算的确定方法	
		培训预算的工作要点	

2. 技能部分

序号	鉴定内容	重要程度
1	搜集、整理、分析培训需求信息	9
2	撰写培训需求分析报告	5
3	培训目标的设定	5
4	培训计划的编制	9
5	培训的组织管理	9
6	培训预算的编制	5

三、练习题

【理论知识部分】

(一) 判断题（下列判断正确的请打"√"，错误的请打"×"）

1. 企业要求具备的理想状态与现实状态之间的差距，就是培训需求。（ ）
2. 培训需求分析主要由两部分工作组成：需求调查和调查实施。（ ）
3. 培训需求调查可以由企业高层管理者、培训主管等发起，也可以通过部门自行申报等形式来收集需求信息。（ ）
4. 培训需求分析是整个培训有效进行的前提，也是制订培训计划的基础。（ ）
5. 企业的发展过程是一个动态的、不断变化的过程，当组织发生变革时，培训计划也要满足这种变化，是培训需求分析的前瞻性分析要求。（ ）
6. 在制订培训计划时，要充分考虑人力资源开发的需要，为人才储备做好基础性工作。（ ）
7. 实行扩张投资战略的公司会比实行其他战略的公司更看重诸如新职业介绍和寻找工作技能方面的培训开发。（ ）
8. 研究表明，同事和管理者对培训开发的支持在员工参与培训开发的热情和动力方面有一定的影响。（ ）

9. 在任务分析中,任务重要性是对员工完成这些任务的能力要求,这在一定程度上反映了从事此项任务的门槛高度。( )
10. 简单地说,人员分析的关键就是找出哪些人员"不愿",哪些人员"不能",这样才能有针对性地设计培训方案。( )
11. 人员分析中的工作结果分析是指员工完成工作的情况。( )
12. 保证人力资源开发系统的有效性是培训需求分析的作用之一。( )
13. 只有对组织的使命有较深刻的理解,才能在培训需求分析时做到有针对性和目标性。( )
14. 从培训需求分析到培训实施,再到培训效果评估,是一个随时与员工沟通的过程。( )
15. 关键事件是指那些对组织目标的实现起较大促进作用或阻碍作用的事件,是工作过程中对组织绩效有重大影响的事件。( )
16. 问卷调查法的主要问题是:对问卷设计的要求较高,被调查者很少有发挥的空间,很难发现新的和更深层面的信息,可能出现低返回率的情况。( )
17. 访谈法操作简单,可以在大范围内开展。( )
18. 关键事件法的成效在相当程度上取决于关键事件的记录情况。( )
19. 观察法取决于观察者的能力,既适用于那些能够通过观察加以了解的工作,也可应用于复杂程度较高的工作。( )
20. 培训组织者必须了解员工的整体绩效大致处于什么水平,这样才能在培训需求分析时保证其科学性。( )
21. 培训目标是指培训活动的目的和预期效果。( )
22. 培训目标中的条件要素是指在什么条件下要达到规定的标准。( )
23. 把一些相关但价值不大的内容罗列在一起,以求丰富培训内容,是企业在组织培训活动中常犯的错误之一。( )
24. 企业培训活动效果评估流于形式的主要原因是没有明确、客观的依据可遵循。( )
25. 投资回报率指培训的货币收益与培训成本的比较,可用来评价组织培训的效益。( )
26. 培训对象在完成培训后应该表现出的行为、行为赖以发生的特定环境条件和组织可以接受的业绩标准,称为培训目标。( )
27. 培训目标的内容要素包括知识的传授、技能的培养等。( )
28. 培训计划必须满足组织及员工两方面的需求,兼顾组织资源条件及员工素质基础,并充分考虑人才培养的超前性及培训结果的不确定性。( )
29. 对于长期培训计划而言,时间过长则对有些变数无法做出预测,时间过短就失去了长期培训计划的意义。( )

30. 中期培训计划起到了承上启下的作用，是长期培训计划的进一步细化，同时又为短期培训计划提供了参照物。（   ）

31. 如果资源有限，可以省略中期培训计划，只保留长期和短期培训计划。（   ）

32. 短期培训计划是指时间跨度在1年以内的培训计划。（   ）

33. 培训者在进行培训前，一定要明确培训的真正意义，并将培训意义与公司的发展、员工的职业生涯紧密地结合起来。（   ）

34. 培训的目标从受训者角度进行理解就是在培训活动结束后应该掌握什么内容。
（   ）

35. 培训计划在实施过程中可能会遇到一些问题，需要在计划完成后进行修订。
（   ）

36. 新技术培训可以避免员工的时间与培训项目日程安排发生冲突。（   ）

37. 培训对象在不同地域且培训交通费用较高时，通常采用在线培训等新技术培训方法。（   ）

38. 培训师的选择是培训工作取得成功的关键，也是培训准备工作的重中之重。
（   ）

39. 内部培训师的来源一般为各级管理人员和各职类职种的业务骨干。（   ）

40. 内部培训师制度也是一种有效激励手段。（   ）

41. 根据培训师的知识和经验、培训技能、个人魅力三个维度，以及"一般"和"好"两种表现，可以将培训师从高到低分为八种类型。（   ）

42. 培训机构的选择步骤包括确定培训目标、与培训机构联系、发出征询建议书、进行挑选、最终确定。（   ）

43. 培训师的来源主要有两个，一是来自组织内部，二是来自组织外部。（   ）

44. 聘用外部培训师可能出现的问题包括：培训师对组织不熟悉，培训工作中的沟通和协调相对比较困难。（   ）

45. 培训预算包括：场地费，食宿费，培训器材、教材费，培训相关人员工资，外聘老师讲课费和交通差旅费。（   ）

46. 为了减少预算时间，应由培训部门独立完成预算编制任务。（   ）

47. 除了直接成本，学员们来参加培训而耽误工作所花费的机会成本也不可忽视。
（   ）

48. 预先确定企业内人均培训经费预算额，再乘以在职人员数量的培训预算决定方法，叫费用总额法。（   ）

49. 在每个预算年度开始时，将所有还在进行的管理活动都看作重新开始，即以零为基础，根据组织目标重新审查每项活动对实现组织目标的意义和效果，并在成本收益分析基础上，重新排出各项管理活动的优先次序，是需求预算法。（   ）

50. 比较外部培训和内部培训，企业内部培训是企业培训的发展方向。（   ）

(二) 单项选择题（下列每题的选项中，只有1个是正确的，请将其代号填在括号中）

1. 培训需求分析的基本目标是（　　）。
   A. 确认培训内容　　　　　　B. 确认差距
   C. 确认需培训的对象　　　　D. 确认培训课程

2. 厘清工作绩效令人不满意的原因，是知识、技术、能力的欠缺，还是个人动机或工作设计方面的问题，是（　　）分析要解决的问题。
   A. 组织层面　　B. 战略层面　　C. 任务层面　　D. 人员层面

3. 确定重要的任务，以及需要在培训开发中加以强调的知识、技能和行为方式，以帮助员工完成任务，是（　　）分析要解决的问题。
   A. 组织层面　　B. 战略层面　　C. 任务层面　　D. 人员层面

4. 对组织、任务和人员三个层面进行分析时，首先要对（　　）进行分析。
   A. 组织层面　　B. 任务层面　　C. 人员层面　　D. 所有层面一起

5. 任务分析是在特定工作岗位的层次上进行的，主要包括查看工作描述和（　　），确定某项工作的业绩产出标准，要达到此产出标准所必须完成的任务，以及完成这些任务所需的知识、技能、行为、态度等。
   A. 工作规范　　B. 技术要求　　C. 任职资格　　D. 工作关系

6. 在进行任务分析时，必须明确两个主要因素，即任务的重要性与（　　）。
   A. 急迫性　　B. 可行性　　C. 水平　　D. 标准

7. 任务分析的结果是重要性高但水平低，则要（　　）。
   A. 及时培训　　B. 重点培训　　C. 选择培训　　D. 选择可不培训

8. 培训需求分析中，（　　）可以让较多的员工参与培训的决策，因而具有更多的沟通、倾诉和激励作用，但也可能导致意见分散，而且与组织动作没有太大的关系。
   A. 问卷调查法　　B. 自我分析法　　C. 访谈法　　D. 测验法

9. 培训目标一般包括三个要素：内容要素、标准要素和（　　）。
   A. 人员要素　　B. 战略要素　　C. 结果要素　　D. 条件要素

10. 在以下几种培训需求分析方法中，（　　）的成本相对较低。
    A. 访谈法　　B. 问卷调查法　　C. 观察法　　D. 头脑风暴法

11. 组织希望员工做什么（绩效），是培训目的的（　　）。
    A. 内容要素　　B. 标准要素　　C. 条件要素　　D. 结果要素

12. 组织期望员工以什么样的标准来做这件事情，是培训目的的（　　）。
    A. 内容要素　　B. 标准要素　　C. 条件要素　　D. 结果要素

13. 衡量员工对培训内容中强调的原理、事实、技术、程序或过程的熟悉程度，是培训成果中的（　　）。
    A. 认知成果　　B. 绩效成果　　C. 技能成果　　D. 投资回报率

14. 评价员工在技术或技能运用以及行为方式上的提高程度，是培训成果中的

( )。

  A. 认知成果　　　B. 绩效成果　　　C. 技能成果　　　D. 投资回报率

 15. 衡量员工对培训项目的感性认识，以及包括个人态度、动机、忍耐力、价值观、顾客定位等在内的情感、心理因素的变化情况，是培训成果中的（　　）。

  A. 认知成果　　　B. 绩效成果　　　C. 感情成果　　　D. 投资回报率

 16. 受训员工的流动率、事故发生率、成本、产量、质量、顾客服务水平等指标的上升或下降情况，是培训成果中的（　　）。

  A. 认知成果　　　B. 绩效成果　　　C. 感情成果　　　D. 投资回报率

 17. 长期培训计划一般指时间跨度为（　　）的培训计划。

  A. 1~2年　　　B. 2~3年　　　C. 3~5年　　　D. 5年以上

 18. 短期培训计划一般指时间跨度为（　　）的培训计划。

  A. 半年内　　　B. 1年内　　　C. 1~2年　　　D. 2~3年

 19. 在选择培训方法时，要把（　　）的考量放在第一位。

  A. 培训目标　　　B. 培训对象　　　C. 培训计划　　　D. 培训预算

 20. 合理制定培训预算应遵循准确性原则、合作原则和（　　）。

  A. 速度原则　　　B. 合理原则　　　C. 量化原则　　　D. 可衡量原则

 21. 当公司进行年末总结和制订下一年度计划时，应该由（　　）确定培训预算的投放原则和培训方针，以保证培训预算"名正言顺"和"钱出有因"。

  A. 公司高层领导　　　　　　　　B. 人力资源部经理

  C. 提出培训的部门负责人　　　　D. 第三方机构

 22. 如果采用在岗培训的方法，则会出现生产力浪费。专家们估计，在岗培训时所浪费的生产力是正常生产时的（　　）倍。

  A. 1　　　B. 2　　　C. 3　　　D. 4

 23. 只有尽可能在预算程序中吸收更多的人，才能更有效地把握公司业务规划和真正的培训需求，从而保证培训预算切实支持公司战略业务发展和员工生涯发展，是（　　）的要求。

  A. 准确性原则　　　B. 合作原则　　　C. 速度原则　　　D. 合理原则

 24. 培训主管部门要争取和发动从领导到广大员工的参与和有效合作，是（　　）的要求。

  A. 准确性原则　　　B. 合作原则　　　C. 速度原则　　　D. 合理原则

 25. 承袭上年度的经费，再加上一定比例的变动，是培训预算编制的（　　）。

  A. 比例预算法　　　B. 零基预算法　　　C. 比较预算法　　　D. 费用总额法

● **(三) 多项选择题**（下列每题的选项中，至少有2个是正确的，请将其代号填在括号中）

 1. 培训需求分析是指在需求调查的基础上，由（　　）等采取各种方法与技术，对组织内部各部门及其成员的目标绩效与能力结构、现有绩效与能力结构等进行比较分析。

  A. 培训主管部门 B. 部门主管人员 C. 员工个人

  D. 公司分管领导 E. 外部专家

2. 培训调查结果分析是用以确定是否需要培训、（　　）等的一种活动或过程。

  A. 谁需要培训 B. 何时需要培训 C. 需要何种培训

  D. 需要多少预算 E. 是否需要外部讲师

3. 可以从（　　）进行培训需求分析。

  A. 组织层面 B. 战略层面 C. 任务层面

  D. 人员层面 E. 技能层面

4. 组织层面的分析包括（　　）等内容。

  A. 明确组织战略导向 B. 了解组织氛围

  C. 了解组织资源 D. 分析组织人员结构

  E. 了解员工绩效

5. 培训需求分析的人员分析，主要分析个体特征、（　　）等。

  A. 工作输入 B. 工作输出 C. 工作结果

  D. 工作业绩 E. 组织人员结构

6. 相对于组织分析和任务分析，人员分析可以采取的方法更多，如观察工作样本、访谈法、问卷调查法、（　　）等。

  A. 测验（工作知识、技能、成就） B. 评定量表

  C. 关键事件法 D. 工作日志

  E. 心理测验法

7. 培训需求分析较好的时机是（　　）。

  A. 行业或相似组织中出现问题时 B. 新设备或新程序引进时

  C. 员工提升和晋级时 D. 利润上升有充足预算时

  E. 新员工入职时

8. 访谈对象可以是（　　）。

  A. 组织的高层管理人员 B. 有关部门的负责人

  C. 某些特殊岗位上的员工 D. 人力资源部经理

  E. 外部专家

9. 关键事件包括（　　）等。

  A. 系统故障 B. 重要客户的获得或流失

  C. 产品的次品率突然上升 D. 员工的主动离职率突然上升

  E. 国家政策发生重大变化

10. 培训目标的内容要素主要可以分为（　　）等几类。

  A. 知识的传授 B. 技能的培养 C. 态度的转变

D. 个性的改变 E. 员工做事标准的设立

11. 培训成果的类别有（　　）等几大类。
    A. 绩效成果　　B. 技能成果　　C. 投资回报率
    D. 感情成果　　E. 文化成果

12. 培训计划是对培训时间、培训地点、（　　）等做出的预先系统设定。
    A. 培训者　　　B. 培训对象　　C. 培训方式
    D. 培训内容　　E. 培训效果

13. 长期培训计划的重要性在于（　　）等。
    A. 明确了组织未来培训的方向
    B. 明确了实现组织发展目标与现实之间的差距在哪里
    C. 为今后组织培训资源的配置预先做规划
    D. 向社会预告组织今后需要的人才标准
    E. 为组织未来的变革做铺垫

14. 在选择培训对象时要考虑的因素包括（　　）。
    A. 学员接受和掌握培训内容的能力
    B. 学员的岗位工作是否有机会使用培训给予的知识和技能
    C. 学员是否有充足的时间接受培训而不影响工作
    D. 学员使用培训中的知识、技能是否能带来团队业绩的提升
    E. 学员短期内离职的可能性

15. 对培训开发方法进行比较和选择一般需要考虑（　　）等因素。
    A. 学习成果　　B. 学习环境　　C. 培训成果转化
    D. 成本　　　　E. 实施难度

16. 培训的组织实施需要考虑的因素包括（　　）。
    A. 培训方法的选择　　　　B. 培训师的选择
    C. 培训机构的选择　　　　D. 培训预算
    E. 培训对象的选择

17. 优秀的培训师具有的特点包括（　　）。
    A. 有培训热情　　　　　　B. 有教学愿望
    C. 受到受训者的尊敬　　　D. 有耐心
    E. 德高望重

18. 优秀的培训师需要具备的能力包括（　　）等。
    A. 学习与创新能力　　　　B. 观察与捕捉能力
    C. 策划与组织能力　　　　D. 引导与应变能力
    E. 动手和实施能力

19. 培训师好坏的评判维度包括（　　）。

A. 知识和经验　　B. 培训技能　　C. 个人魅力
D. 学识学历　　　E. 费用高低

20. 在以下几种培训师中，建议邀请的培训师类型是（　　）。
A. 卓越型培训师　　B. 专业型培训师　　C. 讲师型培训师
D. 弱型培训师　　　E. 敏感型培训师

21. 最好不要邀请（　　）来授课。
A. 演讲型培训师　　B. 讲师型培训师　　C. 敏感型培训师
D. 弱型培训师　　　E. 专业型培训师

22. 来自组织内部的培训师有其特殊的优势，包括（　　）。
A. 能用组织熟悉的语言和事例来解释培训的内容
B. 能让学员容易接受和理解培训内容
C. 深知培训的具体目标
D. 提供的培训更具有针对性
E. 成本低廉

23. 内部培训师制度的内容应包括（　　）。
A. 选拔对象　　　　　　　　B. 选拔流程和选拔标准
C. 任职资格管理　　　　　　D. 讲课酬劳标准
E. 职业晋升标准

24. 聘用外部培训师的优势在于（　　）。
A. 选择余地大
B. 带来全新的视角、理念、信息和风格
C. 提高培训的档次、学员的兴趣和培训的效果
D. 减少内部培训师对正常工作的影响
E. 成本低廉

25. 外部培训师的缺点包括（　　）。
A. 了解组织需求的时间和精力成本高
B. 对组织不熟悉，所传授的内容可能不实用
C. 培训工作中的沟通和协调相对比较困难
D. 费用高
E. 存在泄露企业机密的风险

【技能部分】

案例 1

案例背景

张鹏是一家装备机械制造企业新上任的人力资源部经理，他意识到互联网时代如果公司缺乏互联网思维、计算机应用能力，将无法应对市场的竞争环境，因此安排培训主管小刘编制一份相关的培训计划。公司高层领导非常支持，下拨了十几万元培训费。于是小刘详细规划了"对公司全体人员——上至部门经理，下至一线生产员工，分批进行为期三天的脱产信息化相关培训，包括互联网思维讲座、计算机操作等主题的培训"。

从培训的效果来看，除了办公室的几名行政人员和几位 45 岁以上的中层干部觉得计算机应用能力培训有所收获外，其他人员要么觉得收效甚微，要么觉得学而无用，对什么是互联网思维也是觉得云里雾里，不知所云。员工们议论纷纷，十几万元的培训费用只买来了一时的"轰动效应"。小刘感到非常委屈：在一个传统制造企业，给员工灌输一些新知识、新理念，让员工提升信息技术应用能力为什么效果会不理想呢？

案例思考

1. 该公司的培训效果为什么不理想？
2. 如果你是培训主管，将从哪些层面进行培训需求分析？

案例 2

案例背景

城建公司是一家主要从事城市建筑排水工程设计、安装、咨询及售后服务的专业性公司。城建公司的培训情况为：人力资源部主要根据各部门经理申报的培训申请，制订当年的培训计划。

由于每年都有大量新员工加入，计划中安排的新员工培训，主要是让大家熟悉公司的产品与经营情况，熟悉公司发展历史和规章制度，掌握岗位技能等。由于目前人力资源部人员不够，因此计划中老员工的培训不多，往往选择工作中表现良好的员工参加以传授岗位操作的基本知识和技能为主要内容的培训。对于高层管理者，由于人力资源部感觉其日常管理工作繁忙，因此没有安排培训。培训计划中选择的培训方式是"师带徒"模式和课堂授课方式，培训大都安排在周末，导致员工怨声载道。

人力资源部在与公司高层的交流中了解到，现在的培训对改进公司绩效没有什么明显效果，与培训员工相比，公司更倾向于把经费投入到公司所需人才的招聘上面，从市场上直接招聘人才。

公司培训工作既得不到员工的好评也没能使管理层满意，陷入忙乱而收效甚微的境况中。

案例思考

1. 该公司的培训计划存在哪些问题？

2. 请基于"5W1H"(六何分析法)原理提出培训计划的改进思路。

案例3

案例背景

随着行业竞争加剧,客户要求不断提高,飞天物流公司决定举行一次专题培训,帮助员工提升专业知识水平和解决实际问题的能力。考虑到培训成本和组织实施的便利性,公司培训主管确定了课堂讲授的方式,并通过多方了解,联系到某高校物流专业、在行业内颇有名气的资深教授王教授。

在双休日两天的培训中,王教授时而长篇大论地讲授,时而在白板上画图表演示,授课十分投入,但是讲台下却很混乱。第二天下午课间休息时,学员们聚集在一起议论,仓储主管小李说:"你们觉得这位名师讲的内容与我们的工作有什么相关吗?"货运主管小齐说:"我们经理在培训前可是发话的,受训回岗是有任务的!我们负责运输,我想知道如何处理运输中的突发事故,比如遇到发错货或货物被人做了手脚等。结果听了半天,还没有摸到门道!""这可不行啊,我们可是花了大价钱请他来上课的!平时工作这么忙,能坐到这里听课多不容易啊!"检验员小杨也插话说。

案例思考

1. 该公司在培训组织实施上存在什么问题?
2. 如果你是培训主管,该如何有效进行外部培训师的选择?

四、参考答案

【理论知识部分】

(一) 判断题

1. √ 2. × 3. √ 4. √ 5. √ 6. √ 7. × 8. × 9. × 10. √ 11. × 12. √
13. √ 14. √ 15. √ 16. √ 17. × 18. √ 19. √ 20. √ 21. √ 22. √ 23. √
24. √ 25. √ 26. √ 27. √ 28. √ 29. √ 30. √ 31. × 32. √ 33. √ 34. √
35. × 36. √ 37. √ 38. √ 39. √ 40. √ 41. √ 42. √ 43. √ 44. √ 45. √
46. × 47. √ 48. × 49. × 50. √

(二) 单项选择题

1. B 2. D 3. C 4. A 5. A 6. C 7. A 8. A 9. D 10. B 11. A 12. B 13. A
14. C 15. C 16. B 17. C 18. B 19. A 20. A 21. A 22. D 23. A 24. B 25. A

(三) 多项选择题

1. ABC 2. ABC 3. ACD 4. ABC 5. ABC 6. ABCD 7. ABC 8. ABC 9. ABCD
10. ABC 11. ABCD 12. ABCD 13. ABCD 14. AB 15. ABCD 16. ABCD 17. ABCD
18. ABCD 19. ABC 20. AB 21. BCD 22. ABC 23. ABC 24. ABC 25. ABCD

【技能部分】

案例1

答题思路

1. 培训效果不理想的原因

（1）培训需求分析缺失。人力资源部未能深入研究信息化对公司的价值、对业务的作用和对员工的帮助。

（2）培训对象不合适。没有依据不同职位的工作分析开展针对性的信息化培训。所有内容都进行全员培训缺乏针对性。

（3）培训的方式不合适。从总经理到一线员工，从应届生到中年员工，学习方法、思维方法、接受能力都有较大差异，不适合用同一种方法进行统一培训。

2. 培训需求分析的层面

（1）进行组织层面的培训需求分析。要从组织战略、组织氛围、组织资源角度分析该公司经营发展战略，挖掘信息化对组织发展的价值和需要培训的内容。

（2）进行任务层面的培训需求分析。要从该公司的特定工作岗位和任务出发，分析信息化在管理中的作用，研究信息化相关的培训内容。

（3）进行人员层面的培训需求分析。要根据公司员工绩效要求和未来发展需求确定信息化培训的内容。

案例2

答题思路

1. 培训计划存在的问题

（1）培训计划的目标及意义不够明确。

（2）培训计划中培训对象的选择缺乏针对性，把新员工作为培训重点不太合理，判断老员工与高层管理者是否需要培训和培训什么内容的依据不充分。

（3）培训计划中培训内容简单，以传授岗位操作的基本知识和技能为主，对提升绩效效果不显著。

（4）培训时间安排缺乏灵活性，培训大都安排在周末，影响员工休息，导致员工参与度不高。

（5）培训计划中培训方式仅有"师带徒"模式和课堂授课方式，过于单一，培训转化效果不佳。

2. 培训计划的改进思路

（1）Why——为什么培训，即培训的目的。需要通过有效的培训需求调研，从组织层面、任务层面和个人层面明确培训的意义与目的。这是培训计划的基础和重要内容，需要明确地表述，作为培训的纲领。

（2）Who——培训对象与培训负责人。需要结合培训目的明确培训对象，应该对高层

管理者、老员工和新员工都进行培训。同时，也要明确培训的负责人和组织者。

（3）What——培训什么，即培训内容。需要针对不同对象、不同目标确定合理的培训内容。

（4）When——什么时间培训，即培训时间。应该根据具体的情况进行安排，而不宜统一安排在双休日。

（5）Where——在什么地方培训，即培训地点。需要选择合适的培训地点，进行有效的培训环境布置，有效支持培训实施。

（6）How——如何进行培训。应该针对不同的培训内容，选择合理的培训方式，进一步丰富培训的手段，提高培训的有效性。

案例3

答题思路

1. 该公司在培训组织实施上存在的问题

（1）培训方式过于单一。选择的培训方法不适合培训内容，课堂教学可以满足理论知识方面的培训需求，但在解决工作中的实际问题时有效性不足。

（2）培训师的选择缺乏针对性。没有将培训目标作为第一要素，而将培训成本和实施的便捷性作为培训师选择的第一要素，导致无法达到培训目标。

2. 选择培训师的方法

（1）让培训师做一次试讲或者旁听一次他讲授的相关课程。通过试讲了解培训师的知识储备、经验、培训方式与技能、个人魅力等情况。

（2）索要一份培训师的简历。通过简历信息可以了解培训师的教育、工作、培训等方面的相关经历。

（3）和培训师进行一次面谈或者其他形式的沟通。与培训师探讨培训项目实施的想法和方式，了解其实际水平和对培训项目的了解程度。

（4）请培训师提供一份培训提纲。了解培训师对本次培训的设计规划、讲授思路与方式。

第四单元

绩效管理

绩效管理

一、学习要求

通过本单元的学习,学员应了解和掌握绩效管理的相关知识与技能。本单元重点介绍绩效计划的制订,绩效目标的设定,绩效指标的设计,目标管理法、行为锚定法、关键事件法、360度评估法等主要绩效评估(也称绩效考评、绩效考核)方法的特点和优缺点,绩效评估过程,绩效反馈沟通和绩效结果应用的方法、步骤和注意事项等。

二、职业鉴定考核要点

1. 理论知识部分

鉴定范围	鉴定点	知识点	重要程度
绩效计划	绩效计划的制订	绩效计划及其作用	9
		绩效计划的主要内容	
		绩效计划的相关主体	
		绩效计划的制订原则	
		绩效计划的制订流程	
	绩效目标的设定	绩效目标的含义	5
		绩效目标分解	
		绩效目标确定	
	绩效指标的设计	绩效及其影响因素	9
		绩效指标的要素	
		绩效指标的类型	
		绩效指标设计的原则	
		绩效指标设计的流程	
绩效评估实施	绩效评估方法	目标管理法	9
		行为锚定法	
		关键事件法	
		360度评估法	
	绩效评估过程	绩效评估主体的选择	5
		绩效评估周期的确定	
		绩效评估培训的实施	
		绩效评估结果的评定	
绩效反馈沟通与绩效结果应用	绩效反馈	绩效反馈的含义	9
		绩效面谈	

续表

鉴定范围	鉴定点	知识点	重要程度
绩效反馈与结果应用	绩效申诉机制	绩效申诉的流程	5
		处理绩效评后结果申诉注意事项	
		员工绩效评估结果申诉制度	
	绩效结果应用	绩效评估结果应用的原则	5
		绩效评估结果应用需要防范的问题	
		绩效评估结果应用的范围	
		绩效改进的管理	

2. 技能部分

序号	鉴定内容	重要程度
1	制订绩效计划	5
2	绩效目标的分解	5
3	设计绩效评估表格	9
4	绩效评估的实施	9
5	绩效申诉管理	5
6	绩效面谈	9

三、练习题

【理论知识部分】

● (一) 判断题（下列判断正确的请打"√"，错误的请打"×"）

1. 绩效计划最终落实为订立正式书面协议，即绩效计划和评估表，它是双方在明晰责、权、利的基础上签订的一个内部协议。（　）

2. 员工个人信息的准备工作主要包括员工所在岗位的工作描述和员工个人的绩效表现（上一年度的绩效表现及评估结果）。（　）

3. 绩效计划沟通是计划实施的必要准备工作，不可或缺。（　）

4. 绩效目标应该来源于企业战略，从企业的最高层开始层层分解绩效目标。（　）

5. 个人目标由主管下达，有利于企业绩效目标的实现。（　）

6. 个人目标与部门、组织的目标要始终保持一致，是绩效目标设定的基本要求。（　）

7. 绩效目标需要用"绩效标准＋目标值"来表示。（　）

8. 在绩效目标分解中，可控目标是人员通过努力，只能影响其中的一部分，而无法

全部实现，需由多个部门或多名人员承担的部分。( )
9. 部门可影响目标往往是该部门的关键业绩目标。( )
10. 关键人员流失率目标属于部门可控目标。( )
11. 员工目标分解中包括可控和可影响目标两类。( )
12. 绩效目标设定之后，必须书面确定下来。( )
13. 绩效指标通常包括指标名称、指标定义、标志和标度四个要素。( )
14. 绩效指标的硬指标主要是指通过财务数据进行量化的指标。( )
15. 绩效指标的软指标是难以衡量结果的主观性指标。( )
16. 目标管理法重视和利用员工对组织的贡献，它也是一种潜在有效的评价员工绩效的方法。此方法普遍运用于对专业人员和主管的评价。( )
17. 行为锚定法的重点同时落在绩效结果和工作中表现出来的职能性行为上。( )
18. 行为锚定等级评价法为每种工作设定多个维度，对每个维度都制定独立的评分量表。( )
19. 行为锚定等级评价法由主管及工作承担者共同制定。( )
20. 行为锚定等级评价法的一个主要缺点是设计需要很多时间和工作，而且需为不同的工作制定不同的表格。( )
21. 关键事件法就是常说的 KPI（关键绩效指标）。( )
22. 当这样一种行为对部门的效益产生无论是积极还是消极的重大影响时，主管都应把它记录下来，这样的事件便称为关键事件。( )
23. 关键事件法一般只能作为其他绩效评估方法的一种补充。( )
24. 360 度评估中，来自上级、下属、同事、客户的评估都可能出现偏差。( )
25. 360 度评估一般每年进行一次。( )
26. 绩效评估按主体可分为主管评估、自我评估、同事评估和下属评估。( )
27. 绩效评估可以定期进行，也可以不定期进行。( )
28. 绩效反馈就是评估者将评估结果告知被评估者。( )
29. 绩效反馈实施不当，势必引起员工的不满，员工甚至会猜忌评估结果是否被人调整过。( )
30. 绩效反馈的重要目的之一是就下一个评估周期的目标进行协商。( )
31. 为了避免造成矛盾，绩效反馈时对错误行为的反馈应避免通过正面批评来进行。( )
32. "一个和尚打水喝，两个和尚抬水喝，三个和尚没水喝"的现象，反映出来的是"社会性懈怠"。( )
33. 绩效反馈时，强调个体的表现和贡献，而不是集体荣誉，是一种不当方式。( )
34. 绩效面谈是指管理者要对员工的绩效表现进行打分，确定员工本周期的绩效表

现，然后根据结果，与员工做一对一、面对面的绩效沟通。　　　　　　（　　）

35. 绩效面谈在员工绩效不佳时进行。　　　　　　　　　　　　　　　（　　）

36. 在绩效评估结果应用时，应坚持以人为本，改进和提升员工的能力，促进员工的职业发展。　　　　　　　　　　　　　　　　　　　　　　　　　　　（　　）

37. 员工对绩效评估的结果有异议时，可以提出申诉，人力资源部受理申诉后，必须将所有相关人员召集在一起进行进一步沟通。　　　　　　　　　　　　　（　　）

38. 绩效面谈一般会占用较长时间，所以主管需要提前安排好被评估者的工作。
　　　　　　　　　　　　　　　　　　　　　　　　　　　　　　　　（　　）

39. 缺乏绩效申诉机制可能导致绩效评估前功尽弃。　　　　　　　　　（　　）

40. 被评价人可以通过书面、电子邮件、口头汇报等形式提起绩效申诉。（　　）

41. 绩效评估结果应用范围主要包括制订绩效改进计划，分配薪酬奖金，正确处理内部员工关系等。　　　　　　　　　　　　　　　　　　　　　　　　　（　　）

42. 被申诉人的上级应作为独立的第三方分别与评估人和被评估人面谈，协商并寻求解决纠纷的办法。　　　　　　　　　　　　　　　　　　　　　　　　（　　）

43. 处理完绩效评后结果申诉后，应当及时把令申诉者信服的处理结果告诉员工。
　　　　　　　　　　　　　　　　　　　　　　　　　　　　　　　　（　　）

44. 受理绩效评估结果申诉后，原评价流程暂时中断，但在申诉期间不影响薪酬的调整。　　　　　　　　　　　　　　　　　　　　　　　　　　　　　　（　　）

45. 绩效评估结果应有利于人力资源管理和决策。　　　　　　　　　　（　　）

46. 绩效面谈是指管理者对员工绩效进行打分，然后与员工做一对一或者一对多的面对面的沟通。　　　　　　　　　　　　　　　　　　　　　　　　　　（　　）

47. 绩效评估结果是对员工进行职务调整的重要依据。　　　　　　　　（　　）

48. 绩效评估结果应用包括提供有针对性的培训。　　　　　　　　　　（　　）

49. 正向激励策略与负向激励策略是改进工作绩效的策略。　　　　　　（　　）

50. 通过绩效面谈，确认工作绩效的不足和差距，查明产生的原因，制订并实施有针对性的改进计划和策略，指的是绩效改进计划。　　　　　　　　　　　（　　）

(二) 单项选择题（下列每题的选项中，只有1个是正确的，请将其代号填在括号中）

1. 在绩效计划的准备阶段，需要准备组织信息、部门信息和（　　）。
　　A. 经营目标信息　　B. 企业战略信息　　C. 员工个人信息　　D. 评估信息

2. 在绩效计划的准备阶段，组织信息的准备，主要是对（　　）进行重温和再提高、再认识。
　　A. 个人目标　　B. 团队目标　　C. 组织目标　　D. 部门目标

3. 绩效计划的制订必须与组织和部门的总体目标一致，这是制订绩效计划的（　　）。
　　A. 全员参与原则　　　　　　　　B. 可行性原则
　　C. 目标导向原则　　　　　　　　D. 流程系统化原则

4. 在绩效计划审定和确认阶段,直线经理与( )必须就绩效计划的主要内容进行再次的讨论和确定,保证双方能就内容所规定的各个方面达成共识。
   A. 组织高层管理者   B. 人力资源部
   C. 员工   D. 相关部门经理
5. 员工个人绩效目标的来源包括组织的绩效目标、岗位职责和( )。
   A. 内外部客户的需求   B. 绩效计划的要求
   C. 部门的绩效目标   D. 个人职业发展需求
6. 绩效目标的SMART(关键绩效指标体系)原则中"S"表示( )。
   A. 目标是明确具体的   B. 目标是可衡量的
   C. 目标是可达到的   D. 目标是有时限性的
7. 在影响绩效的四个因素中,( )是最具有主动性、能动性的因素。
   A. 外部环境   B. 内部条件   C. 激励效应   D. 员工技能
8. 通过( ),可以提升员工技能水平,从而提升绩效水平。
   A. 招聘能力更强的员工   B. 技术开发
   C. 加强培训   D. 加大激励力度
9. 平衡计分卡属于( )类型的实施办法。
   A. 相对评价法   B. 绝对评价法   C. 描述法   D. 预测法
10. 全视角评估法(360度评估法)属于( )类型的实施办法。
    A. 相对评价法   B. 绝对评价法   C. 描述法   D. 预测法
11. 强制分配法属于( )类型的实施办法。
    A. 相对评价法   B. 绝对评价法   C. 描述法   D. 预测法
12. 以具体描述的特定工作行为是否被体现为基础来确定员工绩效水平的绩效评估方法,是绩效评估方法中的( )。
    A. 关键绩效指标法   B. 行为锚定法
    C. 描述法   D. 关键事件法
13. 在运用关键事件法的时候,主管人员记录员工的行为,然后定期与员工沟通,周期一般为( )。
    A. 不定期及时沟通   B. 3个月左右
    C. 6个月左右   D. 事先约定的事件发生时
14. 360度评估法的适用人群是( )。
    A. 所有员工   B. 中高层管理者   C. 技术人员   D. 营销人员
15. 360度评估法一般采用( )。
    A. 问卷调查法   B. 访谈法   C. 抽样调查法   D. 相对评估法
16. 绩效评估前需要进行评估培训,培训对象包括管理人员和( )。
    A. 企业中高层管理者   B. 员工

C. 人力资源部工作人员　　　　　D. 需参与评估的客户

17. 在绩效评估结果评定时，由（　　）发放绩效评估表。
    A. 部门经理　　　　　　　　　B. 团队主管
    C. 人力资源部　　　　　　　　D. 直线经理

18. 在绩效反馈时，先对被评估者表现积极的地方进行表扬，然后对其需要改进的工作进行批评指正，最后以肯定和支持结束，是（　　）的沟通技巧。
    A. 胡萝卜加大棒　　　　　　　B. 汉堡原理
    C. BEST 反馈原则　　　　　　D. 笨蛋效应

19. 一个成功的绩效面谈需要事前精心准备，由主管人员和（　　）共同完成。
    A. 人力资源部经理　　　　　　B. 员工
    C. 人力资源部绩效主管　　　　D. 部门经理

20. 在绩效反馈面谈之后，被评价人对自己的评价成绩有异议的，可以向（　　）进行投诉。
    A. 主管　　　　　　　　　　　B. 人力资源部
    C. 主管的上级或人力资源部　　D. 公司领导

21. （　　）应作为独立的第三方分别与评估人和被评估人面谈，协商并寻求解决纠纷的办法。
    A. 人力资源部　　B. 主管的上级　　C. 职工代表　　D. 公司分管领导

22. 接受绩效申诉后，查证工作应在（　　）完成。
    A. 1 周内　　　　B. 2 周内　　　　C. 3 周内　　　D. 1 个月内

23. 绩效评估结果的应用与（　　）紧密结合。
    A. 员工利益　　　B. 主管绩效　　　C. 部门利益　　D. 公司利益

24. 绩效评估结果为组织提供总体人力资源质量优劣程度的确切情况，获得所有人员晋升和发展潜力的数据，服务于组织的（　　）。
    A. 考核制度　　　　　　　　　B. 培训制度
    C. 人力资源规划　　　　　　　D. 招聘和配置计划

25. （　　）不是绩效改进过程中分析工作绩效差距的方法。
    A. 水平比较法　　B. 目标比较法　　C. 横向比较法　　D. 纵向比较法

● **(三) 多项选择题**（下列每题的选项中，至少有 2 个是正确的，请将其代号填在括号中）

1. 绩效管理的内容包括绩效计划、绩效实施、（　　）等。
    A. 绩效评估　　　　　　　　　B. 绩效反馈
    C. 绩效改进　　　　　　　　　D. 绩效评估结果的应用
    E. 奖金计算

2. 绩效计划的主要内容包括员工在绩效评估周期内的主要工作内容、工作职责、所要达到的绩效目的和目的本身的重要性，（　　）等。

  A. 绩效周期结束时，员工所应达到的绩效目标与标准

  B. 员工完成绩效目标的奖惩措施

  C. 为了完成绩效目标，员工所必须接受的培训、辅导或帮助

  D. 收集员工工作绩效的方法和途径

  E. 接受和处理员工对绩效结果的投诉和质疑的程序

3. 绩效计划实施的相关主体包括（　　）等。

  A. 组织高层   B. 组织人力资源专业人员

  C. 管理者   D. 员工个人

  E. IT（信息技术）人员

4. 绩效计划作为绩效管理的一种有效的工具，在制订过程中必须遵守（　　）等原则。

  A. 与组织和部门的总体目标一致

  B. 让员工、管理者和其他相关主体参与到绩效计划的制订过程中

  C. 流程系统化

  D. 贯彻执行

  E. 透明性

5. 绩效计划制订的流程分为（　　）等几个阶段。

  A. 准备阶段   B. 制订阶段

  C. 确认阶段   D. 实施阶段

  E. 修改阶段

6. 绩效计划审定时主要关注（　　）等几个方面。

  A. 绩效计划的内容是否包括员工的主要职责

  B. 指标值的设定是否合理

  C. 绩效计划中的奖惩措施是否到位

  D. 绩效计划的周期是否明确合理

  E. 与员工职级晋升是否有直接关联

7. 绩效目标分解到部门的过程，包括（　　）。

  A. 部门可控目标分解   B. 部门可影响目标分解

  C. 部门目标的横向联系   D. 部门目标的纵向联系

  E. 部门目标的 SMART 分析

8. 影响绩效的主要因素有员工技能、（　　）等。

  A. 外部环境   B. 内部条件   C. 激励效应

  D. 目标设定   E. 企业文化

9. 绩效指标设计的流程包括确定评估对象、进行职责分析、（　　）等。

A. 确定评估指标的大类　　　　　B. 指标的筛选和确定
C. 指标的评估　　　　　　　　　D. 指标的下达
E. 指标的修改

10. 绩效指标的提取依据主要是职责分析的内容、通过框架设计确定的硬指标和软指标，通常采用（　　）等方法提取。

A. 穷举法　　　B. 头脑风暴法　　　C. 问卷调查法
D. 人员访谈法　　E. 无领导小组讨论法

11. 绩效评估实施方法，一般来说有（　　）等几种类型。

A. 相对评价法　　B. 绝对评价法　　C. 描述法
D. 预测法　　　　E. 线性回归法

12. 目标管理实施的步骤包括确定企业目标、确定部门目标、讨论部门目标、（　　）等。

A. 部门领导与下属人员共同确定长期的绩效目标
B. 部门领导将员工实际工作成绩与他们事前商定的预期目标进行比较
C. 定期召开绩效评估会议与下属人员展开讨论
D. 部门领导与员工共同推进目标的完成
E. 解答员工对绩效结果的投诉和质疑

13. 目标管理法的缺点包括（　　）。

A. 重结果，轻过程　　　　　　　B. 目标定位不准确
C. 短期效应较强　　　　　　　　D. 员工对目标无发言权
E. 受到集体合同条款的制约

14. 目标管理法的优点比较明显，包括（　　）等。

A. 操作起来比较简单　　　　　　B. 比较公平
C. 符合绩效管理的目的　　　　　D. 执行力强
E. 员工容易获得晋升

15. 360度评估法的被评估者的信息来源，包括上级、下属、（　　）等。

A. 同事　　　B. 协作部门　　　C. 外部客户
D. 本人　　　E. 外部专家

16. 360度评估法主要用于（　　）等几个方面。

A. 评估被评估者的素质、德行、管理能力等与发展相关的绩效
B. 职业发展，指导对员工的培训、调级、调岗
C. 对中高层管理者进行评估
D. 员工发展潜力评估
E. 加强团队合作，营造和谐文化氛围

17. 360度评估法的内容涉及被评估人员的（　　）等。

A. 任务绩效　　B. 管理绩效　　C. 周边绩效
D. 态度和能力　　E. 专业技能

18. 绩效评估培训的对象包括（　　）。
    A. 管理人员　　　　　　　　B. 部分工作人员
    C. 员工　　　　　　　　　　D. 企业高层管理人员
    E. 统计数据的IT人员

19. 绩效评估结果反馈的原则包括（　　）。
    A. 坚持具体全面原则　　　　B. 互动原则
    C. 对事不对人原则　　　　　D. 奖惩结合原则
    E. 及时性原则

20. 绩效面谈前，主管人员的准备工作包括（　　）。
    A. 收集并准备面谈资料　　　B. 拟订面谈计划
    C. 制订下一步绩效改进计划　D. 选择面谈的时机
    E. 准备提问内容

21. 绩效面谈前，被评估者的准备工作包括（　　）。
    A. 回顾绩效　　　　　　　　B. 准备好下一评估周期的发展计划
    C. 准备好个人提出的问题　　D. 考虑如何提出加薪的要求
    E. 拟订面谈计划

22. 绩效申诉的流程包括提出申诉、（　　）等。
    A. 申诉受理　　　　　　　　B. 查证
    C. 召开申诉处理会议　　　　D. 评估成绩调整
    E. 申诉结果公示

23. 评估结果应用的原则包括（　　）。
    A. 以改进和提升员工的绩效、促进员工的职业发展为目的
    B. 将员工个人的利益与组织群体的利益紧密联系
    C. 评估结果应有利于人力资源的管理和决策
    D. 公开公正透明
    E. 对非相关人员严格保密

24. 评估结果应用中应该避免的问题包括（　　）。
    A. 评估结果没有及时反馈给被评估者
    B. 评估结果没有应用到与员工利益紧密结合的地方
    C. 评估结果的应用没有针对员工需要培训和改进的地方
    D. 评估结果应用方式多样化
    E. 评估结果没有达到预期的效果

25. 评估结果应用的范围主要包括（　　）。

A. 薪酬的分配 B. 职务的晋升调配
C. 个人职业发展计划制订 D. 培训计划制订
E. 人力资源规划的制定

【技能部分】

案例 1

案例背景

启华机器设备有限公司成立仅4年，为了扩大市场规模，更好地鼓励和评价各级员工，在引入市场化用人机制的同时，由人力资源部建立了一套新的绩效管理制度。新制度不但明确了评估的程序和方法，还细化了"德、能、勤、绩"等多项指标，并分别做了定性的描述。但评估结果却出现了问题，工作比较出色的员工，绩效考评成绩未见得较高。

为了弄清这套绩效管理制度存在的问题，王总经理召开部门经理会议，听取本年度公司绩效评估执行情况，对问题进行深入调查。

李经理快人快语："评估指标有十几个，却不能真实反映我们的工作实际，我们部门共有20名员工，需要负责公司60台大型设备的维护工作，工作内容十分繁杂。这么多绩效评估指标，这么多员工，在一周内要完成打分根本来不及，主观性大是必然的。"

韩经理更是急不可待："财务部的工作基本上都是按照会计准则和业务规范来完成的，有些工作无法与'创新能力'这一指标及其评定标准对应。此外，评估中用了传统的民主评议方式，让部门外的人员打分是否恰当？财务工作有些岗位的人员很少和其他部门接触，有些则容易得罪人，让不熟悉的或得罪过的人评估我们，能保证公平公正吗？"

听了大家的各种意见反馈，王总经理陷入了深深的思考之中。

案例思考

1. 该公司的绩效指标设计主要违背了哪些原则？
2. 该公司应该如何进行绩效指标设计工作？

案例 2

案例背景

吴方是洪源公司业务部门的主管，今天他终于费尽心思地完成了对下属员工的绩效评估，并准备把评估表交给人力资源部。绩效评估表中标明了员工的工作数量、工作质量、合作态度等情况，表中的每一个要素都分为5等：优秀、良好、中等、及格和不及格。

今年所有的员工都完成了本职工作。除了小石和小林，其他员工还顺利完成了吴方交给的额外工作。考虑到小石和小林是新员工，他们两人的额外工作量又偏多，吴方给他们的工作量一项都打了优秀。小肖曾经对吴方做出的一个决定表示过不同意见，在合作态度一栏，小肖被计为中等，因为意见分歧只是工作方式方面的问题，所以吴方没有在表格的评价栏上做记录。而小董家庭比较困难，吴方就有意识地提高了对他的评分，他想通过这种方式让小董多拿绩效工资，把帮助落到实处。此外，小陈的工作质量不好，仅达到及格，但为了避免让其难堪，吴方将对小陈的评价提到了中等。

这样，员工的评价分布于优秀、良好、中等3个等级，就没有及格和不及格了。吴方觉得这样做，可以使员工不至于因绩效评估等级低而不满；同时，上级评估时，自己的下级工作做得好，自己的绩效评估成绩也差不了。

案例思考

1. 该公司在组织绩效评估的过程中存在什么问题？
2. 如果你是人力资源主管，将如何改进绩效评估的组织流程？

案例3

案例背景

奇幻数控设备公司年终绩效评估结束后的一天，市场部赵经理在办公室门口遇到了本部门的员工小张。赵经理问小张有没有时间，想利用开会前的几分钟，进行年终绩效反馈沟通。

小张虽然没有准备，但也只能不知所措地接受赵经理的绩效反馈沟通。

赵经理："小张，今年你的业绩总的来说还过得去，但和其他同事比起来还差了许多，但你是我的老部下了，我还是很了解你的，所以我给你的综合评价是3分，怎么样？"

小张："头儿，今年的很多事情你都知道的。我认为我自己还是做得不错的，年初安排到我手里的任务我都完成了……"

赵经理："年初是年初，你也知道公司现在的发展速度。在半年前，部门就接到了新的市场任务，结果到了年底，我们的新任务还差一大截没完成，我的压力也很大！"

这时候，公司总经理办公室小王敲门进来说："赵经理，大家都在会议室里等你呢！"

赵经理："好了，小张，你的工资已经不错了，你看小王的基本工资比你低，工作却比你做得好，所以我想你心理应该平衡了吧。好了，我现在很忙，我们下次再聊。"

小张还想说，但赵经理没有理会小张，匆匆地和小王离开了自己的办公室。

案例思考

1. 赵经理和小张的沟通违背了哪些绩效反馈原则？
2. 如果你是人力资源部主管，你将如何帮助赵经理提高绩效反馈的有效性？

四、参考答案

【理论知识部分】

（一）判断题

1. √ 2. √ 3. √ 4. √ 5. × 6. √ 7. √ 8. × 9. × 10. × 11. √ 12. √
13. √ 14. √ 15. × 16. √ 17. × 18. √ 19. √ 20. √ 21. × 22. √ 23. √
24. √ 25. √ 26. √ 27. √ 28. × 29. √ 30. √ 31. × 32. √ 33. × 34. √

35. × 36. × 37. × 38. × 39. √ 40. × 41. √ 42. × 43. √ 44. × 45. √
46. × 47. √ 48. √ 49. √ 50. √

(二)单项选择题

1. C 2. C 3. C 4. C 5. A 6. A 7. C 8. C 9. B 10. C 11. A 12. B 13. C
14. B 15. A 16. B 17. C 18. B 19. B 20. C 21. A 22. A 23. A 24. C 25. D

(三)多项选择题

1. ABCD 2. ACD 3. BCD 4. ABC 5. AC 6. ABD 7. ABC 8. ABC 9. ABC
10. ABCD 11. ABC 12. BCD 13. ABC 14. ABC 15. ABCD 16. ABC 17. ABCD
18. AC 19. ABC 20. ABCD 21. ABC 22. ABCD 23. ABC 24. ABC 25. ABCD

【技能部分】

案例1

答题思路

1. 该公司的绩效指标设计违背的原则

(1) 违背了客观公正性原则。未能针对具体的岗位提出绩效指标,让不合适的人员进行绩效打分。

(2) 违背了明确具体性原则。指标都是定性指标,界定不明确,标准不清晰,缺乏定量标准。

(3) 违背了数量少而精原则。有些岗位绩效评估指标太多,没有明确关键性指标。

2. 有效开展绩效指标设计的步骤

(1) 确定评估对象并有针对性地进行职责分析,明确工作内容和职责,确定岗位的能力要求,为制定绩效指标提供支持与依据。

(2) 绩效指标体系设计。通过与各部门的沟通提取绩效指标,并进行分析、筛选,确定关键绩效指标。

(3) 通过专家评估等方式进行绩效指标的评估,优化绩效指标,提高绩效指标设定的合理性和可行性。

(4) 根据评估结果进行绩效指标的修正和审核,以获得支持。

案例2

答题思路

1. 该公司在组织绩效评估过程中存在的问题

(1) 绩效评估主体单一。评估主体只有主管,易造成因评估主体单一而评估结果不客观的问题。

(2) 管理人员的绩效评估培训未实施到位,导致主管吴方缺乏评估的正确观念、科学的方法与技术。

(3) 绩效评估结果的评定存在问题。进行评分时,吴方没有以员工的工作成绩与行为事实为依据,没有对各种指标进行科学打分。

2. 绩效评估组织流程的改进

(1) 绩效评估可以采用多主体评估。该公司的评估主体除了主管吴方之外,还可以选择同级、下属或本人自我评估,将结果结合。

(2) 确定绩效评估周期。为了提高评估的科学性和准确性,可以对该部门增加平时评估,定期评估积累资料。

(3) 对管理人员实施绩效评估培训。可以对吴方这样的管理人员实施评估培训,提高管理人员对绩效评估的认识,避免人为误差,掌握必要的方法和技术。

(4) 绩效评估结果评定。要对照绩效协议、工作结果和工作表现评分,要按标准对评估指标打分。

案例3

答题思路

1. 赵经理和小张的沟通中违背的绩效反馈原则

(1) 违背了具体全面的原则。赵经理对小张工作中存在的问题,没有用事实举例说明,导致小张不清楚自己的问题。

(2) 违背了互动原则。在简短的谈话中,赵经理只顾自己说话而不顾小张的诉求,打击了小张参与绩效面谈的积极性。

(3) 违背了对事不对人原则。赵经理面谈的内容没有涉及小张具体做的工作本身,不具有说服力。

(4) 违背了正面引导原则。赵经理没有通过积极、正面的引导,让小张了解自己的不足之处,小张也无法在下一阶段的工作中进行针对性改进。

2. 提高绩效反馈有效性的方法

(1) 收集并准备面谈资料。收集绩效计划、岗位说明书、绩效评估表、被评估者的工作记录等资料。

(2) 拟订面谈计划。赵经理需要编制面谈表,选择面谈时间和地点。

(3) 发放面谈通知书。赵经理需要提前通知小张,以便小张做好面谈准备,填写自我评估表。小张应该对前一段工作进行绩效回顾,对应绩效标准描述工作表现,进行自我评估;应准备下一评估周期的发展计划,准备好要提的问题;应提前安排好工作。

(4) 在绩效反馈过程中,赵经理要与小张建立信任关系,这是有效沟通的前提。赵经理要积极有效地倾听,使用恰当的提问方式,并总结确认小张表述的内容。赵经理的语言表达要使用一定的技巧,避免使用极端化的语言,多使用开放式问题以得到更多信息。

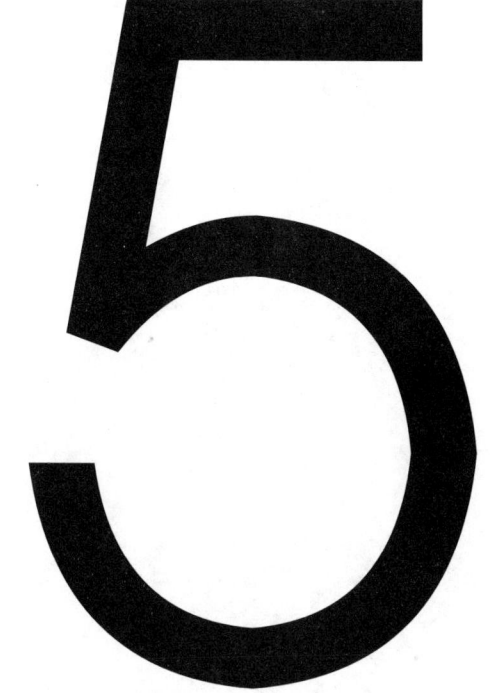

第五单元

薪酬福利管理

一、学习要求

通过本单元的学习,学员应了解和掌握薪酬福利管理的相关知识与技能。本单元重点介绍了薪酬福利管理中的岗位评价、薪酬水平和薪酬结构设计三大块主要工作的知识要点;岗位评价的常用方法,薪酬水平调整的方法和步骤,宽带薪酬体系的设计和应用上的注意事项等。

二、职业鉴定考核要点

1. 理论知识部分

鉴定范围	鉴定点	知识点	重要程度
岗位评价	岗位评价概述	岗位评价的含义	9
		岗位评价的用途	
		岗位评价的原则	
		岗位评价的流程	
	岗位评价方法	排序法	5
		分类套级法	
		要素比较法	
		要素计点法	
		海氏评价法	
薪酬水平	薪酬调查	薪酬调查的目的	5
		薪酬调查的范围	
		薪酬调查的渠道	
		薪酬调查的程序	
	薪酬水平策略	制约薪酬水平的因素	5
		薪酬水平策略的类型	
		薪酬水平策略的选择	
		薪酬水平调整的方法	
		薪酬水平外部竞争力的体现	
薪酬结构设计	薪酬结构设计概述	薪酬结构设计的含义	5
		薪酬结构设计的目的	
		薪酬结构设计的原则	
		薪酬结构设计的流程	

续表

鉴定范围	鉴定点	知识点	重要程度
薪酬结构设计	各类薪酬的结构设计	个体员工薪酬结构设计	5
		不同岗位员工之间的薪酬结构设计	
	宽带薪酬	宽带薪酬概述	5
		宽带薪酬的应用条件	
		宽带薪酬体系的设计	
		实施宽带薪酬应注意的问题	

2. 技能部分

序号	鉴定内容	重要程度
1	岗位评价的流程	9
2	市场薪酬调查	9
3	薪酬满意度调查	5
4	薪酬水平策略选择	5
5	薪酬结构设计	5

三、练习题

【理论知识部分】

● (一) 判断题 (下列判断正确的请打"√",错误的请打"×")

1. 岗位评价又称职位评估或工作评价,是按照一定的客观衡量标准,采用一定的方法,对岗位的性质、难易程度、劳动强度、责任大小、任职资格等进行评价的过程。
(　　)

2. 岗位评价的目的是衡量企业内部每个岗位的价值,并建立各岗位价值间的相对关系。岗位评价的主要依据是工作分析的信息。(　　)

3. 岗位评价主要用于设计薪酬结构和评价任职员工的绩效。(　　)

4. 通过岗位评价,明确了岗位之间的相对价值大小,从而可以为岗位分级分等。
(　　)

5. 让员工积极地参与到岗位评价工作中来,容易让他们对岗位评价的结果产生认同。
(　　)

6. 从总体上来确定不同岗位之间的相对价值顺序的岗位评价方法,是岗位评价的非量化方法。(　　)

7. 排序法是依据工作复杂程度等总体指标对每个岗位的相对价值进行排序。（　）
8. 排序法的优点是将一个岗位与另一个岗位进行比较，在排序方面较易达成共识。（　）
9. 排序法指把岗位按照一系列事先确定好的等级进行分组和归类。（　）
10. 排序法的优点在于快速、简单、费用比较低，而且容易和员工进行沟通。（　）
11. 分类套级法能够快速地对大量的岗位进行评价，在公共部门和企业中仍然有广泛的运用。（　）
12. 要素计点法的缺点在于容易受人的主观影响。（　）
13. 要素计点法在报酬要素的界定、等级定义、点数权重确定等方面都存在一定的主观性。（　）
14. 海氏评价法有效地解决了不同部门的不同职务之间相对价值相互比较和量化的难题。（　）
15. 岗位评价的结果确定了岗位之间的相对价值，从而解决了薪酬水平的问题。（　）
16. 企业的薪酬政策线是为了确保内部薪酬符合国家的相关规定。（　）
17. 内部薪酬调查是针对企业内部薪酬设计的历史演变情况的调查。（　）
18. 外部薪酬调查是针对企业外部、本行业内的薪酬状况进行的调查。（　）
19. 薪酬调查的内容包括长期财务性薪酬和短期财务性薪酬。（　）
20. 薪酬调查要尽可能多地覆盖企业内的岗位。（　）
21. 薪酬调查的基准岗位必须满足两个条件，是组织内具有代表性的岗位，同时也是行业内普遍存在的通用岗位。（　）
22. 从应聘人员那里获得相关企业的薪酬信息是一种不道德的薪酬调查渠道。（　）
23. 进行薪酬调查时，为了充分获取信息，应选择达到目的所必需的尽可能多的企业和岗位。（　）
24. 政府人才交流部门定期发布的岗位薪酬参考信息，由于覆盖面广、薪酬范围大，对有些企业没有意义。（　）
25. 薪酬水平是指企业支付给不同职位的平均薪酬。（　）
26. 企业建立薪酬制度时"对外相对公平，对内有竞争力"的要求在现实操作中经常产生矛盾。（　）
27. 岗位稀缺性、集体工资协议等都是制约薪酬水平的因素。（　）
28. 《工资集体协商试行办法》主要是对企业的约束。（　）
29. 针对不同的部门、不同的岗位、不同的人才，采用不同的薪酬策略，叫差异化薪酬策略。（　）
30. 工资指数化的目的是降低物价波动对员工工资的影响。（　）
31. 控制劳动力成本是企业薪酬外部竞争力的体现。（　）

32. 通过薪酬结构合理设计，达成企业内部各个岗位之间的相对公平，可确保企业合理控制成本，帮助企业有效激励员工。（   ）

33. 薪酬结构设计是指企业中各项工作的相对价值和其对应的实付薪酬之间保持何种关系。（   ）

34. 对外竞争力、对内公平性是薪酬体系设计的基本原则。（   ）

35. 对外竞争力是指薪酬结构与组织层次、职位设计之间形成的对等、协调关系。（   ）

36. 受企业外部环境和内部条件变化的影响，不同职位或技能对企业价值的贡献会发生相应的变化，因此需要定期诊断和调整企业的薪酬结构。这符合薪酬结构设计与组织结构一致的原则。（   ）

37. 当工作任务和流程强调团队合作时，团队中所有成员的薪酬应该尽量缩小差距，以避免破坏合作和因薪酬不公平而产生矛盾。（   ）

38. 当工作流程允许围绕个人任务来组织时，可适度拉大个人间的薪酬差距，并以此作为激励员工绩效的方式。（   ）

39. 各职位等级的薪酬中位值可以根据典型岗位市场薪酬数据，结合岗位评价数值和公司薪酬策略，计算得出。（   ）

40. 岗位工作性质和工作复杂程度与薪酬等级数量关系不大。（   ）

41. 薪酬主要取决于工龄与企业的经营状况，与个人的绩效关联不大，员工收入相对稳定，是折中薪酬模式。（   ）

42. 折中薪酬模式原理合适，但科学合理设计的难度很大。（   ）

43. 稳定薪酬模式适用于稳定经营的企业。（   ）

44. 弹性薪酬模式适用于初创期的企业。（   ）

45. 一岗一薪制的缺点之一是不能进行薪酬调整，尤其是薪酬的个体调整。（   ）

46. 一岗多薪制下，员工薪酬等级的晋升不以岗位晋升为前提。（   ）

47. 职等是指将不同职系中，工作难易繁简程度、工作责任大小、上岗资格条件等相同相似的职级，纳入统一档次，使各个职级之间打破职系的界限产生纵向的平衡关系。（   ）

48. 宽带薪酬的实质就是从原来注重岗位薪酬转变为注重绩效薪酬。（   ）

49. 做好任职资格及薪酬评级工作，可以缓解宽带薪酬给薪酬成本带来的压力。（   ）

50. 汽车制造业是高科技企业，适合宽带薪酬。（   ）

（二）单项选择题（下列每题的选项中，只有1个是正确的，请将其代号填在括号中）

1. 一般多用于部门内岗位评估的方法是（   ）。
   A. 排序法　　　　B. 分类套级法　　　　C. 要素比较法　　　　D. 要素计点法

2. 排序法一般不适用于岗位数量超过（   ）个的情况。

A. 10　　　　　B. 15　　　　　C. 20　　　　　D. 25

3. (　　) 属于量化的岗位评估方法。

   A. 排序法　　　B. 分类套级法　　C. 要素比较法　　D. 回归法

4. 要素比较法需要选择 (　　) 个关键岗位。

   A. 10　　　　　B. 10～15　　　C. 15～20　　　D. 25

5. (　　) 在岗位评价实践中一般不运用。

   A. 排序法　　　B. 分类套级法　　C. 要素比较法　　D. 要素计点法

6. 海氏评价法实质上是一种 (　　)。

   A. 排序法　　　B. 分类套级法　　C. 要素比较法　　D. 要素计点法

7. 下面关于主要的薪酬调查渠道论述最恰当的是 (　　)。

   A. 企业之间相互调查

   B. 从公开的信息中了解

   C. 从其他企业到本企业来的应聘人员也可以了解该企业的薪酬状况

   D. 以上都是

8. (　　) 不属于薪酬调查的内容。

   A. 组织信息　　　　　　　　　B. 薪酬要素信息

   C. 岗位的总体薪酬结构和水平　　D. 薪酬战略

9. (　　) 不是企业薪酬设计要满足的要求。

   A. 外部竞争性　　B. 内部公平性　　C. 合法性　　D. 可控性

10. 对高素质人才需求迫切，企业自身处于高速成长期，薪酬的支付能力比较强，这种情况下一般采用 (　　) 的薪酬水平策略。

    A. 市场领先　　　　　　　　　B. 市场跟随

    C. 成本导向　　　　　　　　　D. 差异化薪酬

11. 实行成本导向战略，考虑尽可能地节约企业生产、经营和管理的成本，这种情况下一般采用 (　　) 的薪酬水平策略。

    A. 市场领先　　　　　　　　　B. 市场跟随

    C. 成本导向　　　　　　　　　D. 差异化薪酬

12. 企业在创业阶段，会采取 (　　) 策略。

    A. 高福利高奖金　　　　　　　B. 低工资低福利，加大长期激励

    C. 与市场水平保持一致　　　　D. 领先薪酬水平

13. 企业处于发展的成熟阶段时，往往采用 (　　) 策略。

    A. 市场领先　　　　　　　　　B. 市场跟随

    C. 滞后　　　　　　　　　　　D. 差异化薪酬

14. 当企业处于再造阶段时，企业应及时调整薪酬水平策略，往往会采用 (　　) 策略。

A. 市场领先 B. 市场跟随
C. 滞后 D. 差异化薪酬

15. （　）不是薪酬水平的外部竞争力的体现方式。
A. 吸引、保留和激励员工 B. 增强企业的实力
C. 塑造企业形象 D. 薪酬水平提高

16. 薪酬固定部分如基本工资、津贴补贴、保险、福利等所占比例较小，浮动部分薪酬如绩效工资、奖金等所占比例较大，是（　）。
A. 稳定薪酬模式 B. 弹性薪酬模式 C. 折中薪酬模式 D. 可变薪酬模式

17. 一般情况下企业会采取（　），即薪酬主要取决于任职者岗位和绩效状况，与团队、个人的绩效有一定关联，员工大部分收入相对稳定。
A. 稳定薪酬模式 B. 弹性薪酬模式 C. 折中薪酬模式 D. 可变薪酬模式

18. （　）的员工流动率最大。
A. 稳定薪酬模式 B. 弹性薪酬模式 C. 折中薪酬模式 D. 可变薪酬模式

19. （　）的员工忠诚度最高。
A. 稳定薪酬模式 B. 弹性薪酬模式 C. 折中薪酬模式 D. 可变薪酬模式

20. 标准化程度高、技术较为单一、工作结果产出统一、岗位比较稳定的岗位或企业员工，比如生产线上的工人等，适合（　）。
A. 一岗一薪制 B. 一岗多薪制 C. 宽带薪酬制 D. 多岗一薪制

21. 在实践中，企业薪酬等级系列平均为（　）级。
A. 7～10 B. 10～15
C. 15～20 D. 20～25

22. 传统等级制薪酬的薪酬带宽一般为（　）。
A. 50%以下 B. 50%～80% C. 80%～100% D. 100%～150%

23. 宽带薪酬的薪酬带宽一般为（　）。
A. 50%～80% B. 80%～100% C. 100%～150% D. 不低于200%

24. 对宽带薪酬的描述不正确的是（　）。
A. 良好的绩效管理是宽带薪酬制度应用的基础
B. 技术型、创新型的企业尤为适合宽带薪酬
C. 成熟的管理队伍必不可少
D. 创业初期企业适合宽带薪酬

25. （　）适合采用宽带薪酬。
A. 创业期企业 B. 汽车厂 C. 知名外贸企业 D. 银行

（三）多项选择题（下列每题的选项中，至少有 2 个是正确的，请将其代号填在括号中）

1. 岗位评价的目的包括（　　）。
   A. 确定岗位的绝对价值　　　　B. 确定职位级别
   C. 为确定员工晋升资格提供依据　D. 为员工职业发展提供参照
   E. 评价员工绩效

2. 岗位评价的原则包括（　　）。
   A. 体现公司战略发展方向
   B. 对岗不对人
   C. 岗位评价的结果应该公开
   D. 让员工积极地参与到岗位评估工作中来
   E. 体现公司绩效导向

3. 岗位评价的流程包括（　　）。
   A. 成立岗位评价小组　　　　B. 选择岗位评价方法
   C. 进行工作分析　　　　　　D. 确定岗位等级
   E. 公示岗位评价结果

4. 岗位评价的方法包括（　　）。
   A. 排序法　　　B. 分类套级法　　　C. 要素比较法
   D. 要素计点法　E. 360 度评估法

5. 排序法的缺点包括（　　）。
   A. 在排序方面很难达成共识
   B. 不能体现岗位之间的差异究竟有多大
   C. 岗位超过一定数量时难度激增
   D. 不同来源和不同工作背景的人不可避免地会在评价过程中夹杂个人的主观意志甚至偏见
   E. 主观性判断比较多

6. 分类套级法的不足之处包括（　　）。
   A. 岗位等级描述容易出现范围过宽或过窄的情形
   B. 可以通过修改或歪曲工作说明书来操纵岗位评价结果
   C. 很难说明不同等级的岗位之间的价值差距到底有多大
   D. 对岗位评价者的培训要求高
   E. 不适合对大数量的岗位进行评价

7. 关键性岗位的特点包括（　　）。
   A. 对员工和组织是非常重要的
   B. 工作要求大致相同

C. 有稳定的工作内容

D. 在薪酬调查中，可以对关键性岗位进行市场调查

E. 岗位数量较少

8. 要素计点法中的付酬因素包括（　　）。

   A. 工作环境　　　B. 岗位所需能力　　C. 工作复杂性

   D. 工作姿势　　　E. 人才获取难易程度

9. 要素计点法包括（　　）等步骤。

   A. 确定待评价岗位的报酬要素

   B. 确定每一个报酬要素在岗位评价体系中所占的权重或者相对价值

   C. 确定每一个报酬要素在内部不同等级或水平上的点值

   D. 将所有被评价岗位根据点值高低排序，建立岗位等级结构

   E. 讨论每一个岗位需要分配多少薪点

10. 在海氏工作评价系统中，所有职务包含的最主要的付酬因素包括（　　）。

    A. 技能水平　　　　　　　　B. 解决问题的能力

    C. 承担的职务责任　　　　　D. 技能稀缺程度

    E. 竞争对手薪酬水平

11. 在海氏工作评价系统的付酬因素中，技能水平包括（　　）等子要素。

    A. 专业理论知识　　　　　　B. 管理诀窍

    C. 人际技能　　　　　　　　D. 职务责任

    E. 沟通职责

12. 要素计点法首先要确定岗位的报酬要素，最常见的报酬要素包括（　　）。

    A. 劳动技能　　B. 劳动强度　　C. 劳动责任

    D. 劳动性质　　E. 劳动力获取成本

13. 企业外部影响薪酬的因素包括（　　）等。

    A. 劳动力市场上人才竞争与供给状况　B. 各行业的薪酬水平

    C. 其他企业的薪酬福利保险项目　　　D. 国家的法律规定

    E. 技术对劳动力的替代

14. 在进行薪酬调查时，要注意的原则包括（　　）等。

    A. 要在被调查企业不知晓的情况下进行调研以获得真实数据

    B. 调查的资料要准确

    C. 调查的资料要随时更新

    D. 要确定岗位职责与本企业的岗位职责完全相同

    E. 不能使用间接资料

15. 外部薪酬调查是针对企业外部市场的薪酬状况进行的调查，要考虑的因素包括（　　）。

A. 企业选择　　　B. 方法选择　　　C. 岗位选择
D. 内容选择　　　E. 调研机构

16. 薪酬调查的基准岗位通常具有（　　）等特征。
    A. 岗位内容众所周知、相对稳定，且得到从事该岗位员工的广泛认可
    B. 岗位的供求不平衡，市场供应短缺
    C. 岗位能代表当前所研究的完整的岗位结构
    D. 岗位上有相当数量的劳动力被雇用
    E. 是企业中的核心稀缺岗位

17. 薪酬调查的内容包括组织信息、岗位基本信息、（　　）等。
    A. 薪酬要素信息　　　　　　B. 调查对象基本信息
    C. 任职者基本信息　　　　　D. 岗位的总体薪酬结构和水平
    E. 政府工资指导线

18. 薪酬调查中最重要的资料是支付给在职者的实际薪酬率，包括（　　）等。
    A. 加薪周期　　　　　　　　B. 工作日长短
    C. 最后增资的日期和幅度　　D. 红利及激励工资
    E. 经济赔偿金支付比例

19. 制约薪酬水平的因素主要包括（　　）。
    A. 劳动力市场价格　　　　　B. 劳资协商谈判结果
    C. 部门和个人绩效　　　　　D. 岗位的价值
    E. 技术对劳动力的替代程度

20. 企业可采取的薪酬水平策略主要有（　　）等。
    A. 市场领先策略　　　　　　B. 市场跟随策略
    C. 成本导向策略　　　　　　D. 差异化薪酬策略
    E. 市场导向策略

21. （　　）等是企业采用的降低薪酬水平的短期措施。
    A. 延缓提薪　　　B. 工资冻结　　　C. 冻结福利项目
    D. 暂停生活补贴　E. 停职留薪

22. 薪酬结构包括（　　）等内容。
    A. 企业工资成本在不同员工之间的分配
    B. 职务和岗位工资率的确定
    C. 员工基本、辅助和浮动工资的比例
    D. 基本工资及奖励工资的调整
    E. 绩效考核对奖金水平的影响

23. 薪酬结构设计应遵循的基本原则包括（　　）。
    A. 与组织目标相符的原则　　B. 按工作流程支付的原则

C. 定期调整的原则　　　　　　D. 兼顾外部竞争性的原则

E. 预算匹配原则

24. 薪酬结构设计流程包括（　　）。

　　A. 确定薪酬最小值、最大值

　　B. 设计工资职等数目

　　C. 设计工资职等中位值及确定职等薪酬增长率

　　D. 设计薪酬幅度、薪级数目及薪级差

　　E. 设计职等升级的标准

25. 宽带薪酬的特征包括（　　）。

　　A. 薪酬等级层次少，浮动范围大

　　B. 薪酬等级最高值与最低值的区间变动比率高

　　C. 为员工提供更多的横向发展空间

　　D. 适用于创业型企业

　　E. 薪酬等级层次多，浮动范围大

【技能部分】

案例1

案例背景

常衡玩具有限公司于2006年成立，员工最初只有几十人。10多年来，由于总经理重视产品的技术研究和市场开发，公司业务发展非常迅速，员工已有1 500多人。公司产品以智能化玩具为主，效益很好，公司也明确了将新一代智能化玩具作为开发重点。

随着组织的发展、部门的扩展、人员的增加，薪酬问题成为很多管理矛盾和人员流失的主要原因。

于是，公司人力资源部开始着手薪酬改革，并进行了岗位评价。人力资源部参考一家外资化工企业的岗位评价报告，通过人力资源部的内部商议排出各岗位的相对价值。在岗位评价讨论中，原来工资较低的行政总监岗位，在参照的化工企业岗位评价报告中的等级较高，但大家认为目前行政总监朱红的综合能力不足，达不到那个等级，所以决定下调行政总监的岗位等级。而在研发总监岗位等级的讨论中，大家虽然觉得研发部对公司影响很大，但其面上的工作强度没有销售部和生产部高，对公司的战略价值无法有效评估，因此其等级定得也不是很高，研发部其他岗位因为工作强度不是很大，评价等级也不高。

岗位评价结果公布后，大家议论纷纷，很多部门对于最终的岗位评价结果不是很满意。

案例思考

1. 该公司在岗位评价中违背了哪些原则？
2. 该公司应如何进行岗位评价？

案例 2

案例背景

普惠公司于 2002 年成立,并于 2010 年改组成股份有限公司。这家起初默默无闻的公司已经成长为国内生产规模最大、技术实力最为雄厚的专业化插座生产企业之一。

公司成立之初,曾以完善的培训体系和富有竞争力的薪酬福利吸引了大批人才的加入,帮助企业迅速崛起。但是近 2 年来,公司内部出现了核心员工离职率大幅上升、一线员工频繁离职的现象。在岗的员工也士气低落,公司产品研发和创新能力大为降低,至 2017 年年末,公司市场份额已大幅下滑。

人力资源部安排主管张晓天开展离职原因调查,发现导致近来员工离职率大幅上升的主要是薪酬问题。研发部原经理离职后在新公司的薪酬是普惠公司的 2 倍;不少员工反映公司薪酬增长太慢,跟不上 CPI(居民消费价格指数)的涨幅;销售部人员也总是抱怨他们拼死拼活在推销产品,薪酬和坐在办公室里的行政人员差不多。而且,由于绩效评估结果都是各部门经理说了算,那些和领导关系比较好的员工奖金比较高,而真正业绩好的员工反而还比不上他们。总经理要求人力资源部立即进行薪酬改革。于是,张晓天被安排先开展薪酬调查。

案例思考

1. 普惠公司的薪酬存在哪些问题?
2. 如果你是人力资源部主管,将如何进行薪酬调查?

案例 3

案例背景

福鼎公司是一家老牌的家用电器生产企业。2009 年小王凭借自身的能力顺利地进入了这家老牌企业。小王非常珍惜这次机会,经常加班加点,赢得了公司上下的一致好评。小王对自己的工资也挺满意,底薪 3 000 元,再加上一些奖金,足够过上相对舒坦的日子了。同一年进入公司的小李和小王是同样的岗位,小李的能力、资历和业绩都不如小王,但按照公司一岗一薪的薪酬结构制度,小李的薪酬与小王相同。小王在和小李的聊天中得知这一情况后,工作积极性一下子受到了极大影响。而小李得知小王的工资后,暗自庆幸自己不那么努力也能得到这样的工资。小王想不通,虽然他们岗位相同,但小李各方面都不如他,相同的工资太不公平了,他何必工作那么努力呢?小王转身就往人力资源部跑去。

案例思考

1. 该公司目前的薪酬结构存在什么问题?
2. 该公司采用什么样的薪酬结构更合理?

四、参考答案

【理论知识部分】

(一) 判断题

1. √ 2. √ 3. × 4. √ 5. √ 6. √ 7. √ 8. × 9. × 10. √ 11. √ 12. ×
13. √ 14. √ 15. × 16. × 17. × 18. × 19. × 20. × 21. √ 22. × 23. ×
24. √ 25. √ 26. × 27. × 28. × 29. × 30. √ 31. √ 32. √ 33. √ 34. √
35. × 36. × 37. √ 38. √ 39. √ 40. × 41. × 42. √ 43. √ 44. √ 45. √
46. √ 47. √ 48. √ 49. √ 50. ×

(二) 单项选择题

1. A 2. B 3. C 4. C 5. C 6. D 7. D 8. D 9. D 10. A 11. C 12. B 13. B
14. A 15. D 16. B 17. C 18. B 19. A 20. A 21. B 22. A 23. D 24. D 25. C

(三) 多项选择题

1. BCD 2. ABCD 3. ABCD 4. ABCD 5. ABCD 6. ABC 7. ACD 8. ABCD
9. ABCD 10. ABC 11. ABC 12. ABC 13. ABC 14. BCD 15. ACD 16. ACD
17. ABCD 18. BCD 19. ABCD 20. ABC 21. ABD 22. ABCD 23. ABD 24. ABCD
25. ABC

【技能部分】

案例 1

答题思路

1. 该公司在岗位评价中违背的原则

(1) 违背了"评价的是岗位而不是岗位中的人"的原则，在岗位评价过程中只考虑人的因素而没有考虑岗位的因素。

(2) 违背了"员工参与岗位评价"的原则，只由人力资源部来决定岗位评价，没有让各级员工积极地参与到岗位评价工作中来，容易导致员工对岗位评价结果的不认同。

(3) 违背了"要体现公司战略发展方向"的原则，没有对企业战略价值重点评价，未体现岗位在企业的战略发展方向上的重要程度。

2. 岗位评价的步骤

(1) 进行工作分析。明确公司的战略和目标，有效分析工作岗位，确定职责、权限、任职资格等，为岗位评价奠定基础。

(2) 成立岗位评价小组。建立由高层领导、人力资源部、各部门管理者、员工甚至外部专家组成的岗位评价小组，形成组织和执行机构，推进岗位评价工作。

(3) 选择岗位评价方法。针对公司自身的特点，而不是简单借助外部公司的成果，进行合理的公司岗位评价。

(4) 进行有效的信息收集、整理和分析。全面收集各类岗位信息，进行汇总、整理和分析，客观有效地确定各个岗位的相对价值大小。

（5）确定岗位等级。汇总岗位评价分析结果信息，进行岗位分级，为后续薪酬设计奠定基础。

案例 2

答题思路

1. 该公司薪酬存在的问题

（1）对外缺乏竞争力，现有薪酬水平显著低于市场上的竞争公司。

（2）对内缺乏激励性，绩效好的员工薪酬水平不高。

（3）部门之间比较，薪酬缺乏公平性，未能体现部门间的价值差异。

2. 薪酬调查的做法

（1）确定调查目的。现有薪酬问题既有内部问题，又有外部问题，因此要进行内外部的薪酬调查。

（2）确定基准岗位。考虑到时间和成本的因素，公司可以针对离职率高的和重点的岗位开展薪酬调查。

（3）确定调查的范围和对象。公司对外可以选择一些具有竞争性的插座生产企业进行薪酬调查，或通过相关咨询公司了解外部薪酬情况，对内可以对相关岗位的员工进行薪酬调查。

（4）确定薪酬调查的内容和项目。该公司可以通过调查问卷调查组织资料，最重要的是调查支付给在职者的实际薪酬率。

（5）选择合适的调查方式，进行薪酬信息收集。公司可以通过访谈和调查问卷采集薪酬数据。

（6）整理、修正和分析调查的薪酬数据。公司调查完后要对收集到的数据进行整理、修正和分析，形成最终的调查结果。

案例 3

答题思路

1. 该公司薪酬结构存在的问题

该公司采用的是一岗一薪制，即每个岗位对应一个确定的工资等级，同岗完全同薪。一岗一薪制虽然简单易行，但不能反映员工能力、资历、绩效，导致了小王的工作积极性受挫和小李的工作不上进，在公平和效率方面均不能激励员工，而且对于小王和小李的问题，一岗一薪制也无法进行个体的薪酬调整。

2. 建议采用的薪酬结构

建议公司采用一岗多薪制，即将岗位薪酬标准设定为一个范围，一个岗位的工资对应几个等级。工资等级可以根据能力确定，也可以根据资历确定，还可以根据业绩确定。如果该公司采用一岗多薪制，则可以实现同岗不同薪，小王的能力、资历、业绩高于同岗位的小李，就可以得到更高等级的工资，对小王和小李更具有激励性。

第六单元

劳动关系管理

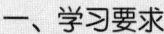

劳动关系管理

一、学习要求

通过本单元的学习,学员应了解和掌握劳动关系管理的相关知识与技能。本单元重点介绍了员工关系管理对企业发展的重要性和做好员工关系管理的方法,国家对于劳动规章制度、集体协商机制、集体合同管理、职工民主管理的法律规定和企业实践中的经验、方法、步骤等。

二、职业鉴定考核要点

1. 理论知识部分

鉴定范围	鉴定点	知识点	重要程度
员工关系管理	员工关系管理概述	员工关系与员工关系管理	5
		员工关系管理的重要性	
		员工手册	
	劳动规章制度制定和实施	劳动规章制度的含义	5
		劳动规章制度的内容	
		劳动规章制度的制定程序	
		劳动规章制度的法律效力	
	劳动纪律制定和实施	劳动纪律的含义	5
		劳动纪律的实施	
		惩戒权的限制	
集体协商机制与集体合同管理	集体协商	集体协商的主体	9
		集体合同协商的过程	
		集体协商注意的环节	
		集体协商的技巧	
	集体合同管理	集体合同的含义	9
		集体合同的特征	
		集体合同的内容	
		集体合同订立的原则	
		集体合同管理的内容	
		集体合同争议处理	
职工民主管理	职工民主管理概述	职工民主管理的概念	5
		职工民主管理的立法	
		职工民主管理的形式	

续表

鉴定范围	鉴定点	知识点	重要程度
职工民主管理	职工代表大会	职工代表大会的性质	9
		职工代表大会的职权	
		职工代表的权利和义务	
		职工代表大会的主要程序	
	工会	工会概述	5
		工会组织	
		工会的权利和义务	

2. 技能部分

序号	鉴定内容	重要程度
1	员工手册的编制	9
2	劳动规章制度的编制	9
3	劳动纪律的管理	5
4	集体协商	5
5	集体合同的编制	5
6	职工民主管理	5

三、练习题

【理论知识部分】

(一) 判断题（下列判断正确的请打"√"，错误的请打"×"）

1. 员工关系指员工与公司、员工与员工之间的关系，就是劳资关系的一个称谓。（ ）

2. 员工关系强调以员工为主体和出发点的企业内部关系，注重个体层次上的关系和交流，关注的是和谐与合作。（ ）

3. 和谐的员工关系是激励员工、减轻工作压力的重要手段之一。（ ）

4. 员工关系管理的主要职责是：协调员工与公司、员工与员工之间的关系，引导建立积极向上的工作环境。（ ）

5. 建设积极有效、健康向上的企业文化，引导员工价值观，维护公司的良好形象，也是员工关系管理的主要内容。（ ）

6. 员工手册是员工关系管理的主要载体。（ ）

7. 劳动规章制度又称企业内部的劳动规章制度，是指用人单位依法制定并在本单位

内部实施的组织劳动和进行劳动管理的规则。( )

8. 企业制定的劳动规章制度调整范围仅限于与企业有劳动契约关系的特定劳动者,不能适用于其他不特定的人。( )

9. 企业制定劳动规章制度,必须经过民主协商程序,兼顾企业与劳动者的合法权益,才能具有法律效力。( )

10. 企业劳动规章制度的法律效力可以溯及以往。( )

11. 劳动纪律是指用人单位依法制定的、全体职工在劳动过程中必须遵守的行为规则。( )

12. 企业规章制度是企业的内部事情,只要不违法,一般不要求将其制定的劳动规章制度报送劳动行政部门备案。( )

13. 劳动纪律的内容一般应当包括时间纪律、组织纪律、岗位纪律、职场纪律等。( )

14. 劳动纪律常见的公示方法包括:公布、培训、员工签字、企业发文、办公会议讨论、职工代表大会通过、内部局域网发布、公证、刊登于内刊厂报等。( )

15. 惩戒处分是指用人单位为保障自身生产经营活动的顺利进行对劳动者违反企业劳动规章制度的行为进行的制裁。( )

16. 劳动纪律应在法律允许的范围和程度内对职工行为进行约束,不得违法限制和剥夺职工依法享有的权利和自由,对违纪职工不得采取法定限额外的惩罚措施,这是劳动纪律的公平平等原则。( )

17. 劳动纪律起草过程中应当征求工会、员工代表意见。( )

18. 为了涵盖一些不能预见的情况,可在劳动纪律中加入"其他严重违反劳动纪律的行为等"的条款。( )

19. 用人单位为保障自身生产经营活动的顺利进行,可以对劳动者违反企业劳动规章制度的行为进行惩戒。( )

20. 制定劳动纪律和惩戒制度是企业依法享有的自主权,但其权利行使受企业规章制度的约束。( )

21. 集体协商又称为集体谈判,是用人单位工会或者职工代表与相应的用人单位代表为签订集体合同进行商谈的行为。( )

22. 集体协商主要采取协商会议的形式,是一种高度规范化、程序化的商谈。( )

23. 集体协商双方的代表中,职工人数应该超过资方。( )

24. 职工一方的协商代表由本单位工会选派。未建立工会的,需先成立工会。( )

25. 职工一方的首席代表由单位工会主席或其委托的其他协商代表担任。( )

26. 集体协商的首席代表可以由非本单位人员代理。( )

27. 为确保集体合同的切实履行和落到实处,集体合同签订后,要选出一批能够代表企业各个层面、确实能够维护职工权益的人员,组成集体合同监督小组,强化履约日常监

督机制。（ ）

28. 签订的集体合同要按规定报送地方劳动行政部门审查，以保证集体合同的有效性。生效的集体合同要报上级工会部门备案。（ ）

29. 集体合同是指全体员工与用人单位或者其团体根据法律、法规、规章的规定，就劳动报酬、工作时间、休息休假、劳动安全卫生、职业培训、保险福利等事项，通过集体协商签订的书面协议。（ ）

30. 集体合同的目的是以全体劳动者的共同利益为中心，明确劳动条件和就业条件，如在劳动报酬、工作时间、福利津贴等方面设定具体标准。（ ）

31. 集体合同的当事人双方的义务具有对等性。（ ）

32. 集体合同是要式合同，是指合同必须按照双方约定的形式、内容和程序签订。（ ）

33. 集体合同与劳动合同具有同等的效力。（ ）

34. 《中华人民共和国劳动法》第三十五条规定：职工个人与企业订立的劳动合同中劳动条件和劳动报酬等标准不得高于集体合同的规定。（ ）

35. 集体合同纠纷是集体合同当事人因签订或履行集体合同而发生的争议。（ ）

36. 职工民主管理又称企业民主管理，是指劳动者直接或间接参与所在企业内部事务的管理，主要形式包括职工大会、职工代表大会或其他形式。（ ）

37. 我国第一次以规章的形式全面规范以职工代表大会为基本形式的企业民主管理制度，是2012年12月中央纪委等六部门共同颁布的《企业民主管理规定》。（ ）

38. 目前我国的职工民主管理仅限于公有制企业。（ ）

39. 工会是我国国有企业实行企业民主管理的最基本形式，是全体职工行使民主管理权力的机构。（ ）

40. 职工代表的构成应当以一线职工为主，中高层管理人员不超过20%。（ ）

41. 跨地区、跨行业的大型集团企业，中高层管理人员在职工代表中的占比不超过20%。（ ）

42. 职工代表大会依法行使的职权包括审议建议、审议通过、民主评议等。（ ）

43. 对于企业的发展规划、重要决策，职工代表大会依法行使审议通过职权。（ ）

44. 对于涉及劳动报酬、工作时间等事项的集体合同草案，职工代表大会依法行使审议建议职权。（ ）

45. 工会的职责主要包括参与和协助。（ ）

46. 工会是职工自愿结合的工人阶级的群众组织，其基本职责是维护职工合法权益。（ ）

47. 工会各级组织按照民主集中制原则建立。（ ）

48. 工会成员不足25人的，不可以单独建立基层工会委员会，而需由几个单位联合组建基层工会委员会。（ ）

49. 当基层工会所在的企业关闭、合并、破产、以其他形式终止，或者所在的机关、事业单位被撤销时，基层工会组织可以撤销。（   ）

50. 工会经费的来源主要是工会会员缴纳的会费。（   ）

（二）单项选择题（下列每题的选项中，只有1个是正确的，请将其代号填在括号中）

1. 员工上岗和离职面谈、人事手续办理、员工申诉和人事纠纷等相关劳动争议处理，属于员工关系管理中的（   ）。
   A. 劳动关系管理　　　　　　　　B. 员工纪律管理
   C. 员工人际关系管理　　　　　　D. 员工绩效管理

2. 组织员工满意度调查、预防及处理员工消极怠工、解决员工关心的问题，属于员工关系管理中的（   ）。
   A. 员工情绪管理　　　　　　　　B. 员工纪律管理
   C. 员工人际关系管理　　　　　　D. 员工绩效管理

3. 不适合作为规章制度的公示方法的是（   ）。
   A. 将劳动规章制度作为劳动合同的组成部分
   B. 将企业劳动规章制度向每位入职员工发放
   C. 以电子邮件和书面公告方式向全体员工公示
   D. 由部门经理向员工进行传达

4. 集体协商双方首席代表可以书面委托本单位以外的专业人员作为本方协商代表。委托人数不得超过本方代表人数的（   ）。
   A. 1/5　　　　B. 1/4　　　　C. 1/3　　　　D. 1/2

5. 生效的集体合同要报（   ）备案。
   A. 地方劳动保障行政部门　　　　B. 上级工会部门
   C. 工会　　　　　　　　　　　　D. 董事会

6. 集体合同的当事人一方是用人单位或者其团体，另一方是（   ）。
   A. 工会　　　　　　　　　　　　B. 职工代表大会
   C. 全体员工　　　　　　　　　　D. 职工代表

7. 职工代表大会或者全体职工讨论集体合同草案或专项集体合同草案，应当有（   ）以上职工代表或者职工出席。
   A. 1/3　　　　B. 1/2　　　　C. 2/3　　　　D. 3/4

8. 集体合同草案或专项集体合同草案必须经全体职工代表或者全体职工的（   ）同意，方获通过。
   A. 2/3以上　　B. 半数以上　　C. 3/4以上　　D. 100%

9. 集体合同或专项集体合同期限一般为（   ）年。
   A. 1　　　　　B. 2　　　　　C. 1～3　　　　D. 1～5

10. 集体合同或专项集体合同期满前（   ）个月内，任何一方均可向对方提出重新签订或续订的要求。

  A. 1   B. 2   C. 3   D. 4

11. 集体合同或专项集体合同签订或变更后，应当自双方首席代表签字之日起（　　），由用人单位一方将文本一式三份报送劳动行政部门审查。

  A. 1 周内   B. 10 日内   C. 2 周内   D. 1 个月内

12. 劳动行政部门对集体合同或专项集体合同有异议的，应当自收到文本之日起（　　）将"审查意见书"送达双方协商代表。

  A. 1 周内   B. 15 日内   C. 20 日内   D. 1 个月内

13. 因履行集体合同发生争议，当事人申请仲裁后，对仲裁裁决不服的，可以自收到仲裁裁决书之日起（　　）向人民法院提起诉讼。

  A. 1 周内   B. 15 日内   C. 20 日内   D. 1 个月内

14. 用人单位需要职工代表大会审议建议的事项为（　　）。

  A. 集体合同草案   B. 企事业单位的发展规划

  C. 薪酬制度   D. 劳动用工管理制度

15. 用人单位需要职工代表大会审议通过的是（　　）。

  A. 企业财务预、决算

  B. 集体合同草案

  C. 企业重组改制方案

  D. 工会与企业就职工薪酬调整进行集体协商的结果

16. 企业、事业单位、机关建立基层工会委员会的条件是工会会员人数在（　　）人以上。

  A. 20   B. 25   C. 30   D. 35

17. 工会经费的来源之一是建立工会组织的企业、事业单位、机关按每月全部职工工资总额的（　　）向工会拨缴的经费。

  A. 2%   B. 3%   C. 4%   D. 5%

18. 基层工会组织可以撤销，撤销时应报告（　　）。

  A. 董事会   B. 劳动行政部门

  C. 上一级工会   D. 职工代表大会

19. （　　）不属于可以撤销基层工会组织的情况。

  A. 所在的企业关闭、合并   B. 所在的企业破产

  C. 所在的机关、事业单位被撤销   D. 工会成员下降到法定数量以下

20. （　　）不是工会的建议权涉及的范畴。

  A. 企业单方面解除职工劳动合同   B. 劳动安全卫生权利

  C. 停工怠工事件   D. 员工奖惩处罚

(三) 多项选择题（下列每题的选项中，至少有 2 个是正确的，请将其代号填在括号中）

1. 从管理职责来看，员工关系管理主要有（　　）等内容。
   A. 劳动关系管理　　　　　　　　B. 员工纪律管理
   C. 员工人际关系管理　　　　　　D. 员工绩效管理
   E. 员工绩效沟通

2. 员工手册编写的原则包括（　　）等。
   A. 依法而行　　　　　　　　　　B. 权责平等
   C. 讲求实际　　　　　　　　　　D. 公平、公正、公开
   E. 透明

3. 员工手册的基本内容包括企业概况、（　　）等。
   A. 企业文化　　B. 组织结构　　C. 人事制度
   D. 行为规范　　E. 员工培训计划

4. 企业劳动规章制度与法律法规不同，其特征主要体现在（　　）等。
   A. 法定授予性　　B. 准立法性　　C. 合法性
   D. 契约性　　　　E. 合规性

5. 劳动规章内容一般包括（　　）。
   A. 劳动条件　　　　　　　　　　B. 劳动纪律
   C. 人事程序管理规定　　　　　　D. 员工绩效管理
   E. 集体合同

6. 相关法律法规对劳动规章制度的制定程序的规定，只针对其中应有的某些环节，即法定环节，主要有（　　）等。
   A. 职工参与　　　　　　　　　　B. 报送审查或备案
   C. 公示或告知劳动者　　　　　　D. 由工会审议通过
   E. 获得全体员工同意

7. 企业规章制度具备效力，需要满足（　　）等条件。
   A. 依法制定
   B. 必须公示明确告知劳动者规章制度的内容
   C. 不得违反劳动合同和集体合同的约定
   D. 必须明确溯及以往的特定条件
   E. 获得工会批准

8. 劳动纪律的制定原则包括（　　）。
   A. 合法原则　　B. 全面系统原则　　C. 公平平等原则
   D. 透明原则　　E. SMART 原则

9. 集体协商的原则包括遵守法律法规等国家规定原则，（　　）等。

A. 相互尊重、平等协商原则　　　　B. 诚实守信、公平合作原则
C. 兼顾双方合法权益原则　　　　　D. 不得采取过激行为原则
E. 全面系统原则

10. 集体合同是工会与用人单位就（　　）等事项签订的书面协议。
A. 劳动报酬　　　B. 工作时间　　　C. 福利津贴
D. 职位升迁　　　E. 职工代表选举办法

11. 集体合同除了具备一般合同的共同特征外，还具有（　　）等特征。
A. 是集体性质的劳动协议
B. 当事人双方的义务具有对等性
C. 是要式合同
D. 效力高于劳动合同
E. 受企业规章制度的约束

12. 双方协商代表协商一致，可以变更或解除集体合同或专项集体合同，但必须符合法定条件，包括（　　）。
A. 用人单位因被兼并、解散、破产等，致使集体合同或专项集体合同无法履行
B. 因不可抗力等致使集体合同或专项集体合同无法履行或部分无法履行
C. 集体合同或专项集体合同约定的变更或解除条件出现
D. 法律法规、规章制度规定的其他情形
E. 获得上级主管部门批准

13. 女职工和未成年工特殊保护主要包括（　　）。
A. 对女职工和未成年工禁忌从事的劳动做出了规定
B. 女职工的经期、孕期、产期和哺乳期的劳动保护
C. 女职工、未成年工定期健康检查
D. 未成年工的使用和登记制度
E. 未成年工合同到期前不得辞退

14. 因履行集体合同发生争议的处理方法有（　　）等几种。
A. 双方协商　　　B. 仲裁　　　C. 诉讼
D. 主管部门裁定　　E. 提交职工代表大会裁决

15. 在我国，（　　）等几种制度并存，共同执行着协调劳动关系的职能。
A. 职工民主管理制度　　　　　B. 劳动合同制度
C. 集体合同制度　　　　　　　D. 劳动争议处理制度
E. 职工代表大会制度

16. 现行职工民主管理的形式主要有（　　）。
A. 通过企业委员会、初级董事会、公司大会、职工代表大会等参与企业管理
B. 职工代表加入企业有关机构或监督企业日常管理活动

C. 职工在劳动岗位上以自治的形式参与企业管理

D. 向企业提出合理化建议

E. 职工代表选举制度

17. 集体合同订立的原则包括合法性、（　　）等。

    A. 自愿性　　　B. 合作性　　　C. 双赢性

    D. 和谐性　　　E. 可追溯性

18. 集体合同的管理包括集体合同订立、（　　）等几项工作。

    A. 变更或解除　　B. 合同终止　　C. 合同审查

    D. 合同公布　　　E. 集体合同废止

19. 职工民主管理的形式主要包括（　　）等。

    A. 组织参与　　B. 代表参与　　C. 岗位参与

    D. 个人参与　　E. 网络投票

20. 工会的职能包括（　　）等。

    A. 参与职能　　　　　　　　B. 协助职能

    C. 监督职能　　　　　　　　D. 参与经营管理职能

    E. 制定规章制度职能

【技能部分】

案例1

案例背景

周海进入程欣公司工作后，双方签订劳动合同的期限为2014年8月至2019年7月。

2015年7月，周海向公司提交书面辞职报告。公司书面通知周海，表示同意其辞职，但需按内部规章制度《关于对专业技术及专业技术管理岗位的部分人员服务期的暂行规定》的有关规定承担违约金、赔偿金等共计人民币15 000余元。

周海不服，认为公司这份暂行规定中，"大中专毕业生进厂需服务5年，提前解除劳动合同的，按服务期每不满一年赔偿违约金2 000元""服务期内提出解除劳动合同的，需承担对工厂生产、经济和工作造成的经济损失5 000元"，是在劳动合同签订以后的规定，之前虽听说过，但具体情况不清楚，自己也没有认可过，因此拒不履行赔偿。

案例思考

1. 该公司依据暂行规定对该员工进行处罚是否合法，为什么？
2. 该公司的人力资源部应如何制定劳动规章制度？

案例2

案例背景

金和军与鑫隆公司签订了为期3年的劳动合同。合同中规定：金和军的工资每月计发一次。合同履行期间，该公司工会与公司经集体协商签订了一份集体合同，该集体合同中规定：职工每年年终可获得一次第 13 个月的工资。

该公司的集体合同获得企业职工代表大会的通过并经当地劳动行政部门审核后开始生效，但年终过后，金和军没有得到公司支付的第 13 个月的工资。于是，金和军向公司提出补发第 13 个月工资的要求。但公司表示，金和军和企业签订的劳动合同中约定了劳动报酬的支付次数，集体合同是企业与工会签订的有关企业综合情况的协议，不应影响劳动合同的履行。双方应当严格按照劳动合同的约定履行，公司对金和军提出的要求不予同意，双方由此产生争议。

之后，随着外部环境和公司内部经营情况的变化，市场萎缩，利润下降，公司觉得按现在的经营情况持续下去，无法继续发放第 13 个月的工资了，于是公司考虑要对集体合同进行变更。

案例思考

1. 你认为该公司是否应该支付年终第 13 个月的工资给金和军，为什么？
2. 该公司是否可以进行集体合同变更？为什么？

案例 3

案例背景

海城公司是一家传统的家居用品制造公司。由于市场竞争的日益激烈，员工不断增加，公司需要进行一系列管理制度的调整。其中，公司高层决定对销售人员薪酬模式进行改革，取消原有职位的薪酬制度，将原有的 4 个级别简化为 2 个级别，分别为销售代表和高级销售代表，中间级别的全部采取降薪处理，以改薪前销售代表的底薪为标准发放，业务提成的比例也有所降低，且显著提高了绩效考核的标准，提高了提成发放的门槛。

为了快速解决问题，公司紧急召开了职工代表大会。目前公司的职工代表中中高层管理人员占 30%，其他 70% 为普通员工，有相当一部分是销售部人员。但由于召开职工代表大会的时候通知得比较匆忙，也正赶上销售的旺季，销售部人员中很多职工代表都不在本地，无法及时参会，其他部分职工代表因各种原因请假，因此出席的职工代表人数是代表总数的 60%。在讨论有关薪酬改革的议题时，由于大家事前没有了解方案的详情，来不及细细分析，虽然有部分员工提出了不同意见，但现场也没有条件提出更具体的依据，最终大会用举手表决的方式，通过了薪酬改革方案。

在薪酬制度执行过程中，销售部人员的反应强烈，认为公司完全不顾员工利益，职工代表大会的程序不合法，薪酬改革方案不合理，但却没有其他正式途径有效反馈。

案例思考

1. 该公司在召开职工代表大会过程中存在哪些问题？
2. 该公司应如何改进民主管理的形式？

四、参考答案

【理论知识部分】

（一）判断题

1. × 2. √ 3. √ 4. √ 5. √ 6. √ 7. √ 8. √ 9. √ 10. × 11. √ 12. ×
13. √ 14. √ 15. √ 16. × 17. √ 18. × 19. √ 20. √ 21. √ 22. √ 23. ×
24. × 25. √ 26. × 27. √ 28. √ 29. × 30. √ 31. × 32. × 33. × 34. ×
35. √ 36. √ 37. √ 38. √ 39. √ 40. √ 41. × 42. √ 43. × 44. × 45. √
46. √ 47. √ 48. × 49. √ 50. ×

（二）单项选择题

1. A 2. A 3. D 4. C 5. B 6. A 7. C 8. B 9. C 10. C 11. B 12. B 13. B
14. B 15. B 16. B 17. A 18. C 19. D 20. D

（三）多项选择题

1. ABC 2. ABCD 3. ABCD 4. ABD 5. ABC 6. ABC 7. ABC 8. ABC
9. ABCD 10. ABC 11. ACD 12. ABCD 13. ABCD 14. ABC 15. ABCD 16. ABCD
17. ABCD 18. ABCD 19. ABCD 20. AB

【技能部分】

案例1

答题思路

1. 该公司的处罚不合法

该公司的暂行规定属于企业内部的规章制度。依据此暂行规定对周海的处罚并不合法，因为有效的劳动规章制度应具备如下要件。

（1）劳动规章制度必须由用人单位依法制定，包括内容合法和程序合法。规章制度内容不得违反劳动法及有关法律法规的强制性规定，法律规定必须经过职代会、职工大会及法律规定的其他民主形式通过的，必须按法定的民主程序制定。

（2）必须公示明确告知劳动者规章制度的内容。未经公示的企业内部劳动规章制度，对职工不具有约束力。

（3）劳动规章制度不得违反劳动合同和集体合同的约定。如果劳动规章制度与劳动合同冲突，除非劳动者认可，否则无效。

（4）企业劳动规章制度的效力不能溯及以往。只对其发布实施之后的人或事产生效力。

案例中的暂行规定不符合上述要件，对周海的处罚也就无效。

2. 人力资源部制定劳动规章制度的步骤

（1）提出人力资源管理制度草案。在拟定起草这类规章制度时，一定要从企业现有的条件和管理水平出发，不能脱离实际。

（2）广泛征求意见，认真组织讨论。规章制度的制定要有职工参与程序，职工认为不适当的，要通过协商予以修改完善。

（3）公示或告知劳动者。人力资源部要对劳动规章制度采用正规、公开的方式予以公示。

案例 2

答题思路

1. 该公司应该支付金和军年终第 13 个月的工资

《中华人民共和国劳动法》规定：职工个人与企业订立的劳动合同中劳动条件和劳动报酬等标准不得低于集体合同的规定。集体合同的效力一般高于劳动合同的效力，无论个别劳动者是否参与谈判，依法定程序产生的由劳动者代表签订的集体合同，合同双方当事人均有义务遵守。《中华人民共和国劳动合同法》规定：依法订立的集体合同对用人单位和劳动者具有约束力。

2. 该公司可以进行集体合同变更

该公司经公司与工会双方协商代表协商一致，可以变更集体合同，但必须符合以下法定条件之一。

（1）用人单位因被兼并、解散、破产等，致使集体合同或专项集体合同无法履行的。

（2）因不可抗力等致使集体合同或专项集体合同无法履行或部分无法履行的。

（3）集体合同或专项集体合同约定的变更或解除条件出现的。

（4）法律、法规、规章规定的其他情形。

案例 3

答题思路

1. 该公司在召开职工代表大会过程中存在的问题

（1）该公司的职工代表构成不合法。职工代表应以一线职工为主体，中高层管理人员不超过 20%，而该公司的中高层管理人员的人数达到了 30%。

（2）该公司参加职工代表大会的职工代表人数未达到法定人数。参会职工代表应超过 2/3，但实际参会人数只有 60%。

（3）对于要讨论的议案没有事前沟通，沟通不够充分，决策形式不够合理。

2. 改进民主管理形式的方法

案例中该公司的民主管理机制不完善，虽然有职工代表大会的形式，但不够完善，缺乏其他途径，需要加强多种形式的职工民主管理。

（1）组织参与。进一步完善职工代表大会的管理机制和规范实施流程，完善代表的比例和开会的规则。

（2）代表参与。通过合法的代表结构促进职工代表参与公司管理。

（3）岗位参与。通过职工在劳动岗位上实行自治的形式使之参与公司管理。

（4）个人参与。通过建立各种个人参与的渠道，提供员工个人参与管理的机会，使员工能够对公司管理提出合理化建议。

第七单元

专业英语

一、学习要求

通过本单元的学习,学员应掌握一定量的人力资源管理专业英语词汇和常用表达方式,学会用英语书面表达人力资源管理工作日常沟通用语。

二、练习题

(一) 英汉互译(请将下面的英语译成汉语,汉语译成英语)

1. absence
2. acceptability
3. achievement test
4. action plan
5. adverse impact
6. allowance
7. announcement
8. applicant
9. application
10. appraisal
11. balanced scorecard
12. bargaining-impasse
13. behavior modeling
14. behavior-based program
15. benchmark
16. candidate
17. career anchor
18. career counseling
19. career curves
20. career development
21. career planning
22. cognitive ability
23. commitment
24. communication skill
25. compensable factor
26. compensation
27. competency assessment

28. competency model
29. competitive advantage
30. compromise
31. concentration strategy
32. consultation
33. continuous learning
34. data flow diagram
35. decentralization
36. decision making
37. deficiency
38. delayering
39. demand forecasting
40. depression
41. development planning system
42. differential piece rate
43. direct compensation
44. direct costs
45. dismiss
46. earnings
47. efficiency wage theory
48. efficiency
49. egalitarian
50. employee empowerment
51. employee leasing
52. employee survey research
53. entrepreneur
54. equal employment opportunity，EEO
55. exit interview
56. expatriate
57. face to face discussion
58. factor comparison system
59. flexibility plan
60. flextime
61. flowchart
62. gain sharing plan

63. goal and timetable
64. group mentoring program
65. head hunter
66. healthy and safety
67. high-performance work system
68. hourly rate
69. hourly work
70. human capital
71. income
72. indirect cost
73. indirect compensation
74. inflation
75. input
76. insurance
77. intellectual asset
78. internal analysis
79. internal growth strategy
80. internal labor force
81. job analysis
82. job classification system
83. job description
84. job design
85. job enlargement
86. job enrichment
87. job evaluation
88. job ranking system
89. key mechanism
90. labor relations process
91. labor turnover
92. leaderless group discussion
93. learning organization
94. manager appraisal
95. management by objectives，MBO
96. managing diversity
97. management forecasts

98. material incentive
99. mediation
100. night shift
101. occupation
102. online training
103. on-the-job training，OJT
104. opportunity to perform
105. organization design and development
106. organizational analysis
107. organization chart
108. organization code
109. panel interview
110. pay claim
111. pay grade
112. pay structure
113. pay-for-performance standard
114. pay-policy line
115. payroll
116. pension
117. peer appraisal
118. performance appraisal
119. performance feedback
120. performance management
121. performance planning and evaluation
122. person specification
123. personnel selection
124. piecework
125. questionnaire
126. readiness for training
127. reasoning ability
128. reconciliation
129. recognition
130. recruitment
131. redundancy
132. reengineering

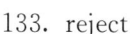

133. reject
134. reinstatement
135. relational database
136. reliability
137. remuneration
138. reputation
139. sick leave
140. self-appraisal
141. social security
142. subcontracting
143. talent
144. situational interview
145. skill-based pay
146. skill inventories
147. selection procedure
148. spot bonus
149. staffing tables
150. strategic choice
151. strategic congruence
152. tacit knowledge
153. task analysis
154. team building
155. total quality management，TQM
156. trade union
157. training administration
158. utility
159. validity
160. verbal comprehension
161. vesting
162. wage and salary survey
163. welfare system
164. wide salary
165. 任命
166. 仲裁
167. 评价中心

168. 评价准则，评估标准
169. 视听教学
170. 审计法
171. 福利
172. 奖金
173. 企业规划
174. 合作培训
175. 核心竞争力
176. 成本结构
177. 关键事件法
178. 跨文化准备
179. 交叉培训
180. 文化环境
181. 文化冲击
182. 顾客评估
183. 差别性对待
184. 多元化培训
185. 红利
186. 歧视
187. 精简
188. 降级
189. 专家系统
190. 显性知识
191. 外部增长策略
192. 外部劳动力市场
193. 首选雇主方案
194. 正规教育计划
195. 参照系
196. 职能工作分析
197. 小组排序法
198. 人力资源信息系统
199. 人力资源管理
200. 人力资源计划
201. 整体的，全盘的
202. 集成，整合性，集成化

203. 实习计划
204. 面试
205. 产业化
206. 内在报酬
207. 工作轮换
208. 工作满意度
209. 工作规范
210. 工作结构
211. 知识型薪酬
212. 直线经理
213. 停工
214. 绩效指南
215. 最低工资
216. 会员资格维持
217. 学习的动机
218. 非营利组织
219. 入职培训
220. 重新谋职
221. 外包
222. 超额工资
223. 权力差距
224. 职位分析问卷调查
225. 潜在资产
226. 项目主管
227. 预测效度
228. 利润分享
229. 晋升
230. 心理契约
231. （核心人员）保持计划
232. 归国准备
233. 替换表
234. 投资回报
235. 角色分析技术
236. 角色扮演
237. 角色转换

238. 客观存在因素

239. 后任

240. 供给预测

241. 战略性人力资源管理

242. 战略执行

243. 下属

244. 可持续发展计划

245. 培训结果

246. 跨国的，超越国界的

247. 趋势分析

248. 离职，流动

249. 发言

250. 就业许可证

(二) 选词填空（请选择正确的单词，将其代号填在横线处，使句子意思完整）

ONE

| A. feedback | B. benchmarking | C. rewards | D. Human resource (HR) management |
| E. benefit | F. on-the-job | G. performance | H. downsizing | I. Direct cost |
| J. output |

1. _____ refers to the practices and policies you need to carry out when handling the people or personnel aspects of your management job.

2. Labor turnover rates provide a valuable means of _____ the effectiveness of HR policies and practices in organizations.

3. Labor turnover can be costly. _____ of recruiting and training replacements should be considered.

4. Business process reengineering techniques are deployed as instruments for _____.

5. Evaluations also fulfill the purpose of providing _____ to employees on how the organization views their performance.

6. The _____ of the job analysis should be a training or learning specification.

7. Coaching is a personal _____ technique designed to develop individual skills, knowledge, and attitudes.

8. Extrinsic _____ include direct compensation, indirect compensation, and nonfinancial rewards.

9. Flexible benefits allow employees to pick and choose from among a menu of

_____ options.

10. China's economic reformers have used material incentives in order to stimulate _____.

TWO

A. promotion	B. job analysis	C. management	D. Globalization
E. job description	F. Human resource planning	G. competence	
H. recruiting	I. mediation	J. assessment	

1. International human resource management includes _____ qualified personnel for overseas assignments.

2. Rapid _____ through an extensive staff ranking system is seen in one company as a very important motivational mechanism.

3. _____ refers to the tendency of firms to extend their sales or manufacturing to new markets abroad.

4. Developing a high-trust organization means creating trust between _____ and employees.

5. _____ determines the human resources required by the organization to achieve its strategic goals.

6. The _____ provides information on the nature and functions of the job.

7. The halo effect or error is the tendency for an evaluator to let the _____ of an individual on one trait influence his or her evaluation of that person on other traits.

8. Training is concerned with fitting people to take on extra responsibilities, increasing all-round _____.

9. A training or a learning specification breaks down the broad duties contained in the _____ into the detailed tasks that must be carried out.

10. In case of labor disputes between the employer and laborers, the parties concerned can apply for _____ or arbitration, bring the case to courts, or settle them through consultation.

THREE

A. reward	B. job analysis	C. human resource management	D. ethics
E. benefit programs	F. human capital	G. agency	H. goals	I. contracts
J. recruiting				

1. For managers, the challenge of fostering intellectual or _____ lies in the fact that such workers must be managed differently from those of previous generations.

2. In summary, _____ is an integral part of every manager's job.

3. In the area of _____ and hiring, it's the line manager's responsibility to specify the qualifications that employees need to fill specific positions.

4. HR manager also administers the various _____ health and accident insurance, retirement, vacation, and so on.

5. Performance evaluations are used as the basis for _____ allocations.

6. Staff managers are authorized to assist and advise line managers in accomplishing these basic _____.

7. Determining the nature of each employee's job is _____.

8. Laborers shall fulfill their tasks of labor, improve their professional skills, follow rules on labor safety and sanitation, and observe labor discipline and professional _____.

9. Labor _____ are agreements reached between laborers and the employer to establish labor relationships and specify the rights, interests and obligations of each party.

10. In a public employment _____, which served workers seeking employment and employers seeking workers, employment interviewers were appraised by the number of interviews they conducted.

FOUR

A. competition	B. arbitration	C. external labor markets	D. careers
E. outplacement	F. job description	G. forecasting	H. expatriate
I. halo effect	J. skills		

1. The analysis of the number of people leaving the organization (labor turnover of wastage) provides data for use in supply _____.

2. Demand forecasting is the process of estimating the future numbers of people required and the likely _____ and competences they will need.

3. The _____ are the external local, regional, national and international markets from which different sorts of people can be recruited.

4. From tapping the global labor force to formulating selection, training, and compensation policies for _____ employees managing globalization will thus be a major HR challenge in the next few years.

5. The pressure for improved performance to meet more intense global _____ explains why many organizations are seeing higher standards for employees.

6. People also leave organizations voluntarily to further their _____, get more money or move away from the district.

7. Organizational release activities deal with redundancy, _____, dismissal, voluntary turnover and retirement.

8. Once a labor dispute occurs, the party that has objections to the ruling of the labor _____ committee can bring the case to a people's court.

9. A training or a learning specification breaks down the broad duties contained in the _____ into the detailed tasks that must be carried out.

10. The _____ is the tendency for an evaluator to let the assessment of an individual on one trait influence his or her evaluation of that person on other traits.

FIVE

A. job satisfaction	B. recruiting	C. organizational learning	D. pay systems
E. strategic plan	F. wage levels	G. motivational	H. needs
I. performance	J. productive		

1. In the management of international joint ventures, Pucik argues that one of the main challenges anywhere is the _____ capacity of the partners within the joint venture.

2. Rapid promotion through an extensive staff ranking system is seen in one company as a very important _____ mechanism.

3. Generally money is seen as important for _____ and retaining employees, but not as a real motivator.

4. China's economic reformers have used material incentives in order to stimulate _____.

5. New labor laws permit companies to set their own _____.

6. Organizations are finding that IHRM activities are best handled by linking them to the enterprise's _____.

7. An extensive review of the literature indicates that the more important factors conductive to _____ include mentally challenging work, equitable rewards, supportive working conditions, and supportive colleagues.

8. Employees want _____ and promotion policies that they perceive as being just unambiguous, and in line with their expectations.

9. The early views on the satisfaction-performance relationship can be essentially summarized in the statement "a happy worker is a _____ worker".

10. Giving all employees the same benefits assumes all employees have the same _____.

SIX

| A. assessment | B. benefits | C. job analysis | D. critical incident |
| E. human capital | F. recruitment | G. selection | H. on-the-job | I. forecasts |
| J. costs |

1. The _____ provides information on the nature and functions of the job.

2. HR is focusing on the acquisition and development of the _____ required by the organization.

3. The downsizing plan should be based on the timing of reductions and of _____ the extent to which these can be achieved by natural wastage or voluntary redundancy.

4. Rapid turnover can result simply from poor _____ or promotion decisions.

5. A flexibility plan can contain proposals to reduce overtime _____ through the use of flexible hours.

6. Job-sharing is an arrangement where by two employees share the work of one full-time position, dividing pay and _____ between them according to the time each works.

7. The _____ plan should include plans for attracting good candidates by ensuring that the organization will become an "employer of choice".

8. Behaviorally anchored rating scales combine major elements from the _____ and graphic rating scale approaches.

9. 360-degree feedback is also referred to as multi-source _____ or multi-rater feedback.

10. Coaching is a personal _____ technique designed to develop individual skills, knowledge, and attitudes.

SEVEN

A. careers	B. money	C. pay levels	D. apprenticeship
E. employment agencies	F. alternative	G. benefit package	H. recruiting
I. contract	J. training

1. The quality of a firm's _____ process had a big impact on what candidates thought of the firm.

2. Private _____ are important sources of clerical, white-collar, and managerial personnel.

3. At Xerox, unionized hourly workers over 55 with 15 years of service and those over 50 with 20 years of service can bid on jobs at lower stress and lower _____ if they desire so.

4. People also leave organizations voluntarily to further their arbitration, get more _____ or move away from the district.

5. Outplacement is about helping redundant employees to find _____ work.

6. Three types of third-party interventions are used to overcome an impasse: mediation, fact-finding, and _____.

7. Approximately half of the German youth between the ages of 15-18 are enrolled in _____ programs.

8. Terms of employment tend to be very technical and are governed by a _____ that spells out exactly what each side will do for the others.

9. Salary and _____ tend to be secret, so no one knows what anyone else is receiving.

10. Every year the company selects dozens of junior managers and young employees to attend universities in order to undertake _____ programs, even degree courses.

EIGHT

A. profit-sharing	B. goals	C. job satisfaction	D. off-the-job
E. skills analysis	F. benefit program	G. interviews	H. outcomes
I. feedback	J. mediation		

1. Job instruction techniques should be based on _____ and learning theory.

2. Desire can be created by amplifying the job's interest factors plus extras such as _____, career development, travel, or similar advantages.

3. Tests, application blanks, and _____ should be a proven part of the employer's selection process.

4. With _____ a neutral third party tries to assist the principals in reaching agreement.

5. Organizational rewards should be linked to each individual employee's _____.

6. The flexible benefits can turn the traditional homogeneous _____ into a motivator.

7. Piece-rate, wage incentive plans, _____, and lump-sum bonuses are all forms of performance-based compensation.

8. Evaluation is the comparison of objectives with _____ to answer the question of how far the training has achieved its purpose.

9. Case study is an _____ training technique.

10. Coaching should provide motivation, structure, and effective _____, if the coacher is skilled, dedicated, and able to develop mutual confidence.

NINE

| A. skills | B. job description | C. interaction | D. management |
| E. role playing | F. work force | G. discipline | H. rewards | I. task |
| J. training |

1. Developing a high-trust organization means creating trust between _____ and employees.

2. Retaining knowledge workers is a matter of providing a supportive workplace environment and motivating them through both tangible and intangible _____.

3. Increased _____ diversity will place tremendous demands on the HR management function.

4. Writing _____ and job specification based on input from department supervisor is the responsibility of HR department.

5. Supervisors should make sure employees are guaranteed fair treatment as it relates to _____, dismissal and job security.

6. It is important to evaluate _____ in order to assess its effectiveness in producing the learning outcomes.

7. Job rotation can be an inefficient and frustrating method of acquiring additional knowledge and _____ unless it is carefully planned and controlled.

8. In _____ the participants act out a situation by assuming the roles of the characters involved.

9. The basis philosophy of managerial grid training is that the _____ of the individual manager is to achieve production through people.

10. Interactive skills training is defined by Rackham as: "Any form of training which aims to increase the effectiveness of an individual's _____ with others."

TEN

| A. workforce | B. absenteeism | C. orientation | D. compensation | E. questionnaire |
| F. downsizing | G. perquisites | H. input | I. performance | J. satisfaction |

1. The appraisal and compensation system is long-term in _____ and based on rewarding people for doing a good job over an extended period of time.

2. The organization will provide employees with indirect compensations insurance, pay for holidays and vacations, services, and _____.

3. Individuals should perceive a strong relationship between their _____ and the rewards they receive if motivation is to be maximized.

4. Wide _____ is a between the salary and salary system of broadband salary system.

5. Satisfied and committed employees have lower rates of turnover and _____.

6. Business process reengineering techniques are deployed as instruments for _____.

7. A forecast is needed of the amount by which the _____ has to be reduced and the likely losses through employee turnover.

8. 360-degree feedback recognizes the complexity of management and the value of _____ from various sources.

9. 360-degree feedback is most likely to be successful when items covered in the _____ can be related to actual events experienced by the individual.

10. When pay is seen as fair based on job demands, individual skill level, and community pay standards, _____ is likely to result.

(三)单项选择题（下列每题的选项中，只有1个是正确的，请将其代号填在横线处）

1. The process of helping redundant employees to find other work or start new careers is _____ .

    A. replacement   B. outplacement   C. release   D. downsizing

2. _____ focus the evaluator's attention on those behaviors that are key in making the difference between executing a job effectively or ineffectively.

    A. The group order ranking   B. Written essay
    C. The individual ranking   D. Critical incidents

3. The _____ plan should include plans for attracting good candidates by ensuring that the organization will become an "employer of choice".

    A. outplacement   B. evaluation   C. recruitment   D. training

4. Organizational _____ and corporate plans indicate the direction in which the organization is going.

    A. goals   B. resource   C. result   D. process

5. _____ aims to broaden experience by moving people from job to job or department to department.

    A. Job analysis   B. Job rotation
    C. Job satisfaction   D. Job involvement

6. HR planning is _____ .

    A. a technique that identifies the critical aspects of a job
    B. the process of determining the human resources required by the organization to achieve its strategic goals

C. the process of setting major organizational objectives and developing comprehensive plans to achieve these objectives

D. the process of determining the primary direction of the firm

7. Career development programs benefit organizations in all of the following ways except _____ .

  A. giving managers more control over their subordinates

  B. giving managers increased skill in managing their own careers

  C. providing greater retention of valued employees

  D. giving an increased understanding of the organization

8. The area from which employers obtain certain types of workers is known as the _____ .

  A. labor market   B. region

  C. recruiting area   D. supply region

9. A set of standards of acceptable conduct and moral judgment is known as _____ .

  A. morals   B. ethics   C. rules   D. legislation

10. Hiring someone outside the company to perform tasks that could be done internally is known as _____ .

  A. outplacement   B. contracting

  C. outsourcing   D. employee leasing

11. The placement of an employee in another job at a higher level in the organization with an increase in pay and status is known as a _____ .

  A. job enlargement   B. transfer   C. promotion   D. job rotation

12. Key jobs have all of the following characteristics except _____ .

  A. they are important to employees and the organization

  B. they vary in terms of job requirements

  C. they are used in salary surveys for wage determination

  D. they are likely to vary in job content over time

13. A process that goes beyond TQM programs to a more comprehensive approach to process redesign is known as _____ .

  A. job redesign   B. process redesign

  C. reengineering   D. rightsizing

14. The job specification describes job requirements relative to _____ .

  A. skill and physical outputs

  B. skill and physical demands

  C. age and physical demands

D. experience and physical description

15. When determining where training emphasis should be placed, an examination of the goals, resources, and environment of the organization is known as _____.

    A. task analysis   B. organization analysis

    C. resource analysis   D. skills analysis

16. The job evaluation system in which specific elements of the jobs to be evaluated are compared against similar elements of key jobs within the organization is known as _____.

    A. the point method   B. job ranking

    C. the comparison method   D. the Hay profile method

17. The final decision to hire an applicant usually belongs to _____.

    A. the HR recruiter   B. the HR manager

    C. line management   D. co-workers

18. Determining what the content of a training program should be, based on a study of the job duties, is known as _____.

    A. organization analysis   B. individual analysis

    C. job analysis   D. task analysis

19. Sometimes organizations provide services to terminated employees that help them bridge the gap between their old position and a new job. These services are known as _____.

    A. downsizing programs

    B. "headhunting" assistance programs

    C. outplacement assistance

    D. employee assistance programs (EAPs)

20. Job _____ form the basis for the administration of applicable employment tests.

    A. outlines   B. specifications   C. requirements   D. details

21. The tendency for an evaluator to let the assessment of an individual on one trait influence his or her evaluation of that person on other traits is known as _____.

    A. similarity error   B. halo effect or error

    C. leniency error   D. single criterion

22. The performance evaluation approach which compares each employee with every other employee and rates each as either the superior or the weaker member of the pair is known as _____.

    A. the paired comparison   B. the individual ranking

C. the group order ranking   D. critical incidents

23. Determining whether or not task performance is acceptable and studying the characteristics of individuals and groups that will be placed in the training environment are known as _____.

    A. person analysis   B. demographic analysis

    C. individual analysis   D. group and individual analysis

24. The lines of advancement for an individual within an organization are known as _____.

    A. career paths   B. job progressions

    C. career lines   D. job paths

25. Freedom from criterion deficiency of performance appraisals refers to the extent to which _____.

    A. standards relate to the overall objectives of the organization

    B. standards capture the entire range of an employee's responsibilities

    C. individuals tend to maintain a certain level of performance over time

    D. factors outside the employee's control can influence performance

26. Which three factors does the Hay profile method use for evaluating jobs? _____.

    A. Knowledge, skill, and responsibility

    B. Mental ability, skill, and responsibility

    C. Knowledge, mental ability, and responsibility

    D. Knowledge, mental ability, and accountability

27. Which of the following is not an important component of a meaningful gainsharing plan? _____.

    A. Establishing fair and precise measurement standards

    B. Ensuring that bonus payout formulas are easy to calculate

    C. Ensuring that bonus payouts are large enough to encourage future employee effort

    D. Depending on top management to develop the gainsharing program

28. Giving employees more control over decisions about who their co-workers will be is known as _____.

    A. empowered selection   B. collaboration

    C. team selection   D. group development

29. Which of the following is a technique used to elicit employee views in order to make decisions and initiate change? _____.

A. Suggestion system   B. Downward communication

C. Attitude survey   D. Empowerment

30. Assessing the degree to which what employees learned during the training program is translated into enhanced employee performance is known as _____ .

A. results evaluation   B. reaction evaluation

C. behavior evaluation   D. learning evaluation

31. Eliminating what are deemed to be unnecessary layers of management and supervision is known as _____ .

A. delayering   B. downsizing   C. right sizing   D. benchmarking

32. The changing environments of Human Resource Management include the following except _____ .

A. work force diversity

B. technological trends

C. globalization

D. great changes in the nature of work force

33. The aims of human resource planning in any organization might be the following except _____ .

A. attract and retain the number of people required with the appropriate skills, expertise and competences

B. reduce dependence on external recruitment when key skills are in short supply by formulating retention, as well as employee development, strategies

C. neglect the problems of potential surpluses or deficits of people

D. develop a well-trained and flexible workforce, thus contributing to the organization's ability to adapt to an uncertain and changing environment

34. Forcasting the supply of people should be based on the following except _____ .

A. forecast losses to existing resources through attrition

B. recruitment plans

C. the effect of changing conditions of work

D. sources of supply from external labor markets

35. The costs of labor turnover include the following except _____ .

A. direct cost of recruiting replacements

B. opportunity cost of time spent by HR and line managers in recruitment

C. loss arising from reduced input from new starters until they are fully trained

D. indirect cost of training replacements in the unnecessary skills

36. Assessing the sets of skills and knowledge employees need to be successful, par-

ticularly for decision-oriented and knowledge-intensive jobs, is known as _____.

  A. individual assessment   B. competency assessment

  C. organizational assessment   D. job assessment

37. Which system of job evaluation is being used when jobs are classified according to a series of predetermined wage grades? _____.

  A. Hay profile method   B. Job ranking

  C. Factor comparison method   D. Job classification system

38. The purpose of a profit-sharing plan is to _____.

  A. allow workers to contribute specific knowledge to improve the organization

  B. motivate a total commitment to the organization as a whole

  C. enable workers to share in labor cost savings

  D. instill commitment to the employees' immediate work group

39. One of the primary benefits of cross-training employees is that _____.

  A. cross-training enables individuals to exert more effort on their jobs

  B. cross-training helps employees identify trouble spots that cut across several jobs

  C. cross-training enables managers to spend less time supervising individual performance

  D. cross-training enables managers to save more money in labor costs

40. Which of the following is not an approach used by organizations to try to lower labor costs? _____.

  A. Downsizing   B. Outsourcing

  C. Productivity enhancements   D. Employee development

41. An interview in which an applicant is given a hypothetical incident and is asked how he or she would respond to it is a _____.

  A. computer interview   B. panel interview

  C. situational interview   D. nondirective interview

42. The desired outcomes of training programs are formally stated as _____.

  A. training goals   B. learning objectives

  C. instructional objectives   D. learning goals

43. Career counseling involves talking with employees about all of the following except _____.

  A. their current job activities and performance

  B. their past career decisions

  C. their personal and career interests and goals

D. their personal skills

44. In most instances, who is in the best position to perform the function of appraising an employee's performance? _____ .

A. Someone from the HR department

B. The employee's supervisor

C. The employee

D. Co-workers

45. The process of determining the relative worth of jobs in order to determine pay rates for different jobs is known as _____ .

A. job determination   B. job diagnosis

C. job analysis   D. job evaluation

46. Profit sharing refers to any procedure by which an employer pays employees _____ .

A. an incentive based on their merit

B. an incentive based on labor cost savings

C. a bonus based on the overall productivity of their particular work group

D. current or deferred sums based on the organization's financial performance

47. All of the following are prevalent reasons for failure among expatriates except _____ .

A. a spouse's inability to adapt

B. a manager's personality

C. inability to cope with larger responsibilities

D. distaste for travel

48. Communication systems should provide accurate information regarding all of the following except _____ .

A. business plans and goals

B. employee background and personal data

C. unit and corporate operating results

D. incipient problems and opportunities

49. Reengineering often requires that managers start from scratch in rethinking all of the following except _____ .

A. how work should be done

B. how technology and people should interact

C. how the entire organization should be structured

D. how organizations should compete

50. The core job dimension that describes the degree to which a job has a substantial impact on the lives or work of other people is called _____.

  A. skill variety   B. task identity

  C. task significance   D. autonomy

51. Questions contained in structured job interviews should be based on _____.

  A. job analysis   B. job design

  C. job specialization   D. job utilization

52. A process in which individuals are evaluated as they participate in a series of situations that resemble what they might be called upon to handle on the job is known as a/an _____.

  A. management training seminar   B. executive development program

  C. in-basket exercise   D. assessment center

53. If your primary objective for a performance appraisal is to give employees developmental feedback, which of the following appraisal methods should you use? _____.

  A. Trait method   B. Results method

  C. Behavior method   D. Attitudinal method

54. Outplacement services are _____.

  A. useful methods of attracting individuals into a career

  B. designed to help terminated employees find a job elsewhere

  C. rarely given to executive employees

  D. vital parts of any career management system

55. Transnational teams tend to be _____.

  A. focused on projects that span multiple countries

  B. comprised of members with generalized skills

  C. homogenous

  D. comprised of members from the same region

56. Which of the following compensation systems does not focus employee efforts on outcomes that are beneficial to both themselves and the organization as a whole? _____.

  A. Profit-sharing plans   B. Employee stock ownership plans

  C. Hourly based pay systems   D. Skill-based pay systems

57. The total-quality HR paradigm would likely emphasize all of the following except _____.

  A. cross-functional training

  B. team/group-based rewards

  C. autocratic leadership

D. customer and peer performance reviews

58. A group of employees rotating jobs as they complete the production or service process is called a/an _____ .

    A. labor bargaining unit   B. employee team
    C. training-production group   D. employee rotation unit

59. Notifying applicants of the selection decision and making job offers are generally the responsibility of _____ .

    A. the HR department   B. the line manager
    C. the supervisor   D. the industrial relations manager

60. Performance appraisals are used most widely as a basis for _____ .

    A. determining training needs
    B. discharging decisions
    C. deciding compensation
    D. directing performance improvement

61. All of the following are basic skills needed for successful career management except _____ .

    A. developing a positive attitude
    B. establishing goals
    C. adopting the mindset of your superiors
    D. putting responsibility for your career in the hands of your supervisor

62. Which training method focuses upon learning at the affective level? _____ .

    A. Sensitivity training   B. Apprenticeship training
    C. Intercultural motivation   D. Multilingual training

63. Which of the following facets of organizational training efforts does a total-quality paradigm tends to emphasize? _____ .

    A. Job-related skills   B. Cross-functional skills
    C. Functional, technical skills   D. A narrow range of skills

64. Performance appraisal methods can be broadly classified as either _____, _____, or _____ approaches.

    A. trait, behavioral, judgmental
    B. trait, behavioral, results
    C. behavioral, judgmental, results
    D. behavioral, judgmental, attitudinal

65. When managers talk about "going global" they have to balance a complicated set of issues that include all of the following except _____ .

A. geographical differences   B. cultural differences

C. legal differences   D. personal differences

66. The selection procedure usually begins with _____ .

A. employment tests   B. a medical examination

C. a supervisory interview   D. completion of an application form

67. It is recommended that a diagnosis of poor employee performance focus on all of the following except _____ .

A. skill   B. personality

C. effort   D. external conditions

68. When employees receive a higher rate of pay for all of their work if production exceeds a standard level of output, under which incentive plan are they working? _____ .

A. Differential piece rate   B. Standard piece rate

C. Exception bonus rate   D. Individual rate pay

69. Cultural environment includes all of the following except _____ .

A. education/human capital   B. values/ideologies

C. corporate structure   D. religious beliefs

70. Conducting job analysis is usually the primary responsibility of the _____ .

A. job incumbent   B. line supervisors

C. accounting department   D. HR department

71. The placement of an employee in another job for which the duties, responsibilities, status, and remuneration are approximately equal to those of the previous job is known as a _____ .

A. promotion   B. transfer

C. lateral move   D. job rotation

72. If employees' pay is not based on the actual amount of time, it takes them to complete a job but on a predetermined amount of time for completing the job, which incentive plan are they working under? _____ .

A. Piece-rate plan   B. Standard hour plan

C. Time division plan   D. Completion pay system

73. Of the following, the one that would not be considered a chief objective of most benefits programs is _____ .

A. reducing turnover

B. improving employee satisfaction

C. "sidestepping" legal requirements for employee health and safety

D. attracting and motivating employees

74. The term used to refer to the language, religion, values and attitudes, politics, technology, education, and social organization of a nation is _____.

  A. ritual environment   B. general environment

  C. cultural environment   D. task environment

75. Which of the following is not a typical method of increasing the power of employees? _____.

  A. Job enlargement   B. Enrichment

  C. Standardization   D. Relying on self-managed teams

76. Which management group has primary responsibility for the development of disciplinary policies and procedures? _____.

  A. The legal department   B. Top-level management

  C. The HR department   D. Middle management

77. Which of the following is not a phase of a system model of training? _____.

  A. Needs assessment   B. Motivation assessment

  C. Program implementation   D. Evaluation

78. Which of the following is not a primary impact that technology has had on HRM? _____.

  A. It has altered the methods of collecting employment information

  B. It has sped up the processing of employment data

  C. It has diminished the role of supervisors in managing employees

  D. It has improved the processes of internal and external communications

79. A pictorial representation of all organizational jobs along with the numbers of employees currently occupying those jobs and future employment requirements is called _____.

  A. a staffing table   B. an organization chart

  C. a skills inventory   D. career planning

80. When determining where training emphasis should be placed, an examination of the goals, resources, and environment of the organization is known as _____.

  A. task analysis   B. organization analysis

  C. resource analysis   D. skills analysis

81. An example of a qualitative approach to demand forecasting is _____.

  A. trend analysis   B. the Delphi technique

  C. multiple predictive models   D. modeling

82. Services that are offered to employees who are being transferred to different locations are known as _____.

A. outplacement services B. relocation services
C. transfer services D. adjustment services

83. Self-appraisals are best for _____ .

    A. administrative purposes B. developmental purposes
    C. promotional purposes D. regulatory purposes

84. The point system permits jobs to be evaluated on the basis of elements known as _____ .

    A. description factors B. compensable factors
    C. skill factors D. knowledge factors

85. Sometimes organizations provide services to terminated employees that help them bridge the gap between their old position and a new job. These services are known as _____ .

    A. downsizing programs
    B. "headhunting" assistance programs
    C. outplacement assistance
    D. employee assistance programs (EAPs)

86. Consultation provided by HR staff should not _____ .

    A. be based on managerial expertise
    B. be based on technical expertise
    C. help managers or supervisors make firm decisions
    D. conflict with the goals of the managers or supervisors seeking assistance

87. The examination of the attitudes and activities of a company's workforce refers to _____ .

    A. environmental scanning B. performing a trend analysis
    C. performing a cultural audit D. behavioral modeling

88. When a combination salary and commission plan is used to compensate sales employees, the percentage of cash compensation paid in commission is called _____ .

    A. a bonus B. a lump-sum bonus
    C. an incentive D. leverage

89. The two principal criteria for determining promotions are _____ .

    A. seniority and salary B. knowledge and skills
    C. seniority and knowledge D. merit and seniority

90. When the multinational corporation sends employees from its home country, these employees are referred to as _____ .

    A. host-country nationals B. third-country nationals

C. international managers D. expatriates

91. Executives or managers who coach, advise, and encourage employees of lesser rank are called _____.

A. proteges B. teachers C. mentors D. role models

92. Objectives accomplished through job analysis include all of the following except _____.

A. establishing the job-relatedness of selection requirements

B. determining the relative worth of a job

C. eliminating discrepancies between internal wage rates and market rates

D. proving criteria for evaluating the performance of an employee

93. Staffing the organization, designing jobs and teams, developing skillful employees, identifying approaches for improving employee performance, and other "HRM" issues are duties typically reserved for _____.

A. HR managers B. line managers

C. HR and line managers D. top executives

94. 360-degree feedback might be used for the following except _____.

A. personal development B. appraisal

C. pay D. recruitment

95. An employer wishing to set up the job classification system of job evaluation would have to _____.

A. establish a point plan to evaluate all jobs

B. rank jobs according to the beliefs of committee members

C. describe job grades with increasing amount of responsibility, skill, knowledge, or ability

D. evaluate jobs with the use of a job evaluation scale

96. Which of the following isn't a form of performance-based compensation? _____.

A. Piece-rate B. Profit-sharing

C. Minimum wage D. Lump-sum bonuses

97. The performance measures that might be used for performance-based compensation include the following except _____.

A. individual work time

B. departmental productivity

C. unit profitability

D. the overall organization's profitability

98. Coaching is a _____ technique that can be used to develop individual skills, knowledge, and attitudes.

  A. on-the-job   B. off-the-job

  C. web-based training   D. classroom training

99. Which pay system would an organization wishing to establish greater job-staffing flexibility likely use ? _____ .

  A. Straight pay   B. Skill-based pay

  C. Incentive pay   D. Two-tier pay

100. Human capital of a firm include the following except _____ .

  A. the knowledge of a firm's workers

  B. skills of a firm's workers

  C. the expertise of a firm's workers

  D. the behavior of a firm's workers

（四）阅读理解（阅读以下短文并做短文后面的单项选择题）

ONE

The context for obtaining the people required will be the labor markets in which the organization is operating which are：

（1）The internal labor market—the stocks and flows of people within the organization who can be promoted, trained, or re-deployed to meet future needs.

（2）The external labor marker—the external local, regional, national and international markets from which different sorts of people can be recruited. There are usually a number of markets, and the labor supply in these markets may vary considerably. Likely shortages will need to be identified so that steps can be taken to deal with them, for example by developing a more attractive "employment proposition".

As part of the human resource planning process, an organization may have to formulate "make or buy" policy decisions. A "make" policy means that organization prefers to recruit people at a junior level or as trainee, and rely mainly on promotion from within and training programs to meet future needs. A "buy" policy means that more reliance will be placed on recruiting from outside—"bringing fresh blood into the organization". In practice, organizations tend to mix the two choices together to varying degrees, depending on the situation of the firm and the type of people involves. A highly entrepreneurial company operating in the turbulent conditions, or one which has just started up, will probably rely almost entirely on external recruitment. When dealing with knowledge workers, there may be little choice—they tend to be much more mobile, and resourcing strategy may have to recognize that external recruitment will be the main source of supply. Management consultancies typically fall into this category. Firms which can predict people requirements fairly and accurately may rely more on developing their own staff once they have been recruited.

1. A "make" policy means that organization prefers to promote people from _____ .

    A. regional labor market   B. national labor market

    C. internal labor market   D. international labor market

2. According to the passage, management consultancies _____ .

    A. are less mobile than people at a junior level

    B. should be recruited from external labor market

    C. should be promoted from within the organization

    D. are not knowledge workers

3. If a firm can predict people requirements fairly accurately, it may not _____ .

    A. develop their own staff

    B. formulate training programs

    C. promote people from within the organization

    D. rely more on recruiting from outside

4. "Make or buy" policy decision is a part of _____ .

    A. human resource planning   B. training and development

    C. performance appraisal   D. job analysis

5. The best title of this passage is _____ .

    A. The Organizational Context of Human Resource Planning

    B. Aims of Human Resource Planning

    C. The Labor Market Context for Human Resource Planning

    D. Limitations of Human Resource Planning

TWO

Walters identifies nine sources of information which help to identify training priorities. These are:

(1) Organizational goals and corporate plans which indicate the direction in which the organization is going and, therefore, major training priorities.

(2) Human resource and succession planning which provides information on future skill requirements and management training needs.

(3) Personnel statistics on, for example, labor turnover, which highlight HR issues which might be addressed by training.

(4) Exit interviews which might suggest deficiencies in training arrangements.

(5) Consultation with senior managers which obtains opinions on training needs from key decision makers.

(6) Data on productivity, quality and performance which show where there are any gaps between expectations and results or negative trends, and therefore suggest training needs.

(7) Departmental layout changes which provide information about future developments and related training needs.

(8) Management requests for training which set out perceived needs.

(9) Knowledge of financial plans which determine whether the funds will be available for training, and may encourage fresh approaches if resources are limited.

Two other sources not directly mentioned by Walters are plans for introducing new technology or developing IT systems, and marketing plans which indicate where new skills are required to market new products or services, use different selling techniques or operate in new territories.

1. According to Walters, _____ are major training priorities.

    A. human resource and succession planning

    B. personnel statistics

    C. exit interviews

    D. organizational goals and corporate plans

2. Human resource and succession planning provides information on _____.

    A. the direction in which the organization is going

    B. future skill requirements and management training needs

    C. deficiencies in training arrangements

    D. any gaps between expectations and results or negative trends

3. The following sources of information which help to identify training priorities are mentioned by Walters except _____.

    A. marketing plans

    B. departmental layout changes

    C. data on productivity, quality and performance

    D. consultation with senior managers

4. According to the passage, the following statements are true except _____.

    A. departmental layout changes which provide information about future developments and related training needs

    B. exit interviews highlight HR issues which might be addressed by training

C. data on productivity, quality and performance show where there are any gaps between expectations and results or negative trends

D. marketing plans indicate where new skills are required to market new products or services

5. The main topic about this passage is illustrating _____ .

A. sources of information which provide information on management training needs

B. sources of information of major training priorities

C. sources of information which help to identify training priorities

D. sources of information which provide information about future developments and related training needs

THREE

Multiperson comparisons evaluate one individual's performance against one or more others. It is a relative rather than an absolute measuring device. The three most popular comparisons are group order ranking, individual ranking, and paired comparisons.

The group order ranking requires the evaluator to place employees into a particular classification, such as top one-fifth or second one-fifth. This method is often used in recommending students to graduate schools. Evaluators are asked to rank the student in the top five percent, the next five percent, the next fifteen percent, and so forth. But when used by managers to appraise employees, managers deal with all their subordinates. Therefore, if a rater has twenty subordinates, only four can be in the top fifth, and of course, four must also be relegated to the bottom fifth.

The individual ranking approach rank orders of employees from best to worst. If the manager is required to appraise thirty subordinates, this approach assumes that the difference between the first and second employee is the same as that between the twenty-first and twenty-second. Even though some of the employees may be closely grouped, this approach allows for no ties. The result is a clean ordering of employees, from the highest performer down to the lowest.

The paired comparison approach compares each employee with every other employee and rates each as either the superior or the weaker member of the pair. After all paired comparisons are made, each employee is assigned a summary ranking based on the number of superior scores he or she achieved. This approach ensures that each employee is compared against every other, but it can obviously become unwieldy when many employees are being compared.

Multiperson comparisons can be combined with one of the other methods to blend the best from both absolute and relative standards. For example, a college might use the graphic rating scale and the individual ranking method to provide more accurate information about its students' performance. The A, B, C, D, or E. A prospective employer or graduate school could then look at two students who each got a "B" in their different financial accounting courses and draw considerably different conclusions about each where next to one grade it says "ranked fourth out of twenty-six", while the other says "ranked seventeenth out of thirty". Obviously, the latter instructor gives out a lot more high grades!

1. Multiperson comparisons is a (an) _____ measuring device.

   A. absolute   B. relative   C. accurate   D. false

2. According to the passage, there are three most popular comparisons except _____.

   A. group order ranking   B. individual ranking
   C. graphic rating scales   D. paired comparisons

3. From this passage, we can infer that _____.

   A. recommending students to graduate schools often uses individual ranking
   B. the paired comparison approach assumes that the difference between the first and second employee is same
   C. group order ranking ensures that each employee is compared against every other
   D. each method of multiperson comparisons can be used simultaneously

4. The following statements about individual ranking are false except _____.

   A. it rank orders of employees from the lowest performer up to the highest
   B. the result is a clean ordering of employees
   C. it assumes that the difference between the first and second employee is different
   D. this approach allows for some of the employees who may be closely grouped

5. This article might be extracted from the paper about _____.

   A. performance appraisal   B. recruitment and replacement
   C. training and development   D. reward systems

FOUR

Our knowledge of motivation tells us that people do what they want to satisfy needs. Before they do anything, they look for the payoff or rewards. Many of these rewards—salary increases, employee benefits, preferred job assignments—are organizationally controlled.

The types of rewards that an organization can allocate are more complex than what is generally thought. Obviously, there is direct compensation. But there are also indirect compensation and nonfinancial rewards. Each of these types of rewards can be distributed on an individual, group, or organization wide basis.

Intrinsic rewards are those that individuals receive for themselves. They are largely a result of the worker's satisfaction with his or her job. Techniques like job enrichment or any efforts to redesign or restructure work to increase personal worth to the employee may make his or her work more intrinsically rewarding.

Extrinsic rewards include direct compensation, indirect compensation, and nonfinancial rewards. Of course, an employee expects some forms of direct compensation: a basic wage or salary, overtime and holiday premium pay, bonuses based on performance, profit sharing, and/or possibly opportunities to purchase stock options. Employees will expect their direct compensation generally to align with their assessment of their contribution to the organization, and additionally, will expect it to be comparable to the direct compensation given to other employees with similar abilities and performance.

The organization will provide employees with indirect compensations: insurance, pay for holidays and vacations, services, and perquisites. In as much as these are generally made uniformly available to all employees at a given job level, regardless of performance, they are really not motivating rewards. However, where indirect compensation is controllable by management and is used to reward performance, then it clearly needs to be considered as a motivating reward.

1. Rewards are often considered as a _____ function in human resource management.

    A. planning   B. leading   C. motivating   D. controlling

2. Extrinsic rewards include the following except _____ .

    A. job enrichment   B. direct compensation

    C. indirect compensation   D. nonfinancial rewards

3. According to the passage, the following statements are false except _____ .

    A. nonfinancial rewards belong to intrinsic rewards

    B. overtime and holiday premium pay belongs to indirect compensation

    C. employees will expect their direct compensation to be comparable to the indirect compensation given to other employees with similar abilities and performance

    D. employees will expect their direct compensation generally to align with their assessment of their contribution to the organization

4. Perquisites which the organization provides employees belong to _____ .

A. intrinsic rewards   B. direct compensation
C. indirect compensation   D. nonfinancial rewards

5. The author of this passage would most likely agree that _____ .

   A. if indirect compensation is controllable by management, then it can't be considered as a motivating reward
   B. if indirect compensations are made uniformly available to all employees at a given job level, regardless of performance, they will lose their motivating function
   C. techniques like job enrichment or nonfinancial rewards to increase personal worth to the employee may make his or her work more intrinsically rewarding
   D. each type of rewards can be distributed on an individual or group, not organization wide basis

FIVE

A training or a learning specification is a product of job analysis. It breaks down the broad duties contained in the job description into the detailed tasks that must be carried out. It then sets out the characteristics or attributes that the individual should have in order to perform these tasks successfully. These characteristics are:

Knowledge—what the individual needs to know. It may be professional, technical or commercial knowledge. Or it may be about the commercial, economic, or market environment; the machines to be operated; the materials or equipment to be used or the procedures to be followed; or the customers, clients, colleagues and subordinates he or she is in contact with and the factors that affect their behavior. Or it may refer to the problems that occur and how they should be dealt with.

Skills—what the individual needs to be able to do if results are to be achieved and knowledge is to be used effectively. Skills are built progressively by repeated training or other experience. They may be manual, intellectual or mental, perceptual or social.

Competences—the behaviors' competences needed to achieve the levels of performance required.

Attitudes—the disposition to behave or to perform in a way that is in accordance with the requirements of the work.

Performance standards—what the fully competent individual has to be able to achieve.

1. A training or a learning specification is a product of _____ .
   A. job structure   B. job evaluation   C. job design   D. job analysis

2. According to this passage, which of the following isn't the characteristic or attribute that the individual should have in order to perform the task successfully? _____ .

　　A. Knowledge　　B. Mental ability　　C. Competences　D. Attitudes

3. According to this passage, the knowledge that the individual should have in order to perform the task successfully may include the following except _____ .

　　A. professional, technical or commercial knowledge
　　B. knowledge about the commercial, economic, or market environment
　　C. knowledge about the job description
　　D. the problems that occur and how they should be dealt with

4. From this passage, we can infer that _____ .

　　A. in order to perform tasks successfully, individuals need know more than their professional knowledge
　　B. in order to perform tasks successfully, skills that the individual should have are built only by repeated training
　　C. in order to perform tasks successfully, the disposition to behave or to perform in a way needn't be in accordance with the requirements of the work
　　D. in order to perform tasks successfully, performance standards should be based on what the average individual has to be able to achieve

5. The best title of this passage is _____ .

　　A. Job Analysis
　　B. Training or Learning Specification
　　C. Job Description
　　D. Performance Standards

SIX

Supply forecasting measures the number of people likely to be available from within and outside the organization, having allowed for <u>attrition</u>, absenteeism, internal movements and promotions, and changes in hours and other conditions of work. The forecast will be based on: an analysis of existing human resources in terms of numbers in each occupation, skills and potentials; forecast losses to existing resources through attrition (the analysis of labor wastage is an important aspect of human resource planning, because it provides the basis for plans to improve retention rates); forecast changes to existing resources through internal promotions; the effect of changing conditions of work and absenteeism; sources of supply from within the organization; sources of supply from outside the organization in the national and local labor markets.

Mathematical modeling techniques aided by computers can help in the preparation of supply forecasts in situations where comprehensive and reliable data on stocks and flows be provided. As this is rarely the case, they are seldom used.

The demand and supply forecasts can then be analyzed to determine whether there are any deficits or surplus. This provides the basis for recruitment, retention, and if unavoidable, downsizing plans. Computerized planning models can be used for this purpose. It is, however, not essential to rely on a software planning package. The basic forecasting calculations can be carried out with a spreadsheet which, for each occupation where plans need to be made, sets out and calculates the number required as in the following example:

(1) number currently employed　　　　　　　　　　　70
(2) annual wastage rate based on past records　　　　　10%
(3) expected losses during the year　　　　　　　　　　7
(4) balance at end-year　　　　　　　　　　　　　　　63
(5) number required at end-year　　　　　　　　　　　75
(6) number to be obtained during year(=5-4)　　　　　12

1. The word "attrition" in the first paragraph means _____ .
   A. retention rates
   B. supply from within the organization
   C. supply from outside the organization
   D. labor wastage and retirements

2. According to the passage, forcasting the future supply of people should be based on the following except _____ .
   A. forecast losses to existing resources through attrition
   B. forecast changes to existing resources through external movements
   C. the effect of changing conditions of work
   D. sources of supply from external labor markets

3. The author of this passage might disagree that _____ .
   A. the demand and supply forecasts can be analyzed to determine whether there are any deficits or surplus
   B. the demand and supply forecasts can provide the basis for recruitment, retention
   C. the demand and supply forecasts can't provide the basis for downsizing
   D. a spreadsheet can be used for demand and supply forecasting

4. In a company, if people currently employed are 300, annual wastage rate is 20%,

and number required at end-year is 350, then the company should recruit _____.

  A. 100   B. 110   C. 120   D. 130

 5. This passage may be extracted from the paper about _____.

  A. human resource planning

  B. training and development

  C. recruitment and replacement

  D. international human resource management

SEVEN

  Although the notion of human resource planning is well established in the HRM vocabulary, it does not seem to be commonly practiced as a key HR activity. As Rothwell suggests, "apart from isolated examples, there has been little research evidence of increased use or of its success". She explains the gap between theory and practice as arising from: the impact of change and the difficulty of predicting the future— "the need for planning may be in inverse proportion to its feasibility"; the "shifting kaleidoscope" of policy priorities and strategies within organizations; the distrust displayed by many managers of theory or planning—they often prefer pragmatic adaptation to conceptualization; the lack of evidence that human resource planning works.

  Be that as it may, it is difficult to reject out of hand the belief that some attempt should be made broadly to forecast future human resource requirements as a basis for planning and action. On the basis of research conducted by the Institute for Employment Studies, Reilly has suggested a number of reasons why organizations choose to engage in some forms of human resource planning. These fall into the following three groups.

  (1) Planning for substantive reasons, that is, to have a practical effect by optimizing the use of resources and/or making them more flexible, acquiring and nurturing skills that take time to develop, identifying potential problems and minimizing the chances of making a bad decision.

  (2) Planning because of the process benefits, which involves understanding the present in order to confront the future, challenging assumptions and liberating thinking, making explicit decisions which can later be challenged, standing back and providing an overview, and ensuring that long-term thinking is not driven out by short-term focus.

  (3) Planning for organizational reasons, which involves communicating plans so as to obtain support/adherence to them, linking HR plans to business plans so as to influence them, regaining corporate control over operating units, and coordinating and integrating organizational decision-making and actions.

1. According to Rothwell, the gap between human resource planning theory and practice arised from the following except _____ .

   A. the impact of change and the difficulty of predicting the future

   B. the dramatic change of policy priorities and strategies within organizations

   C. the distrust displayed by many managers of theory or planning

   D. the redundance of evidence that human resource planning works

2. According to the passage, which of the following statements is true? _____ .

   A. The definition of human resource planning is not well established

   B. Rothwell suggests there has been no example of success about human resource planning

   C. Human resource planning does not seem to be commonly practiced as a key HR activity

   D. The gap between human resource planning theory and practice is very small

3. Reilly has suggested a number of reasons why organizations choose to engage in some forms of human resource planning, but which of the following is not included? _____ .

   A. Planning has a theoretical effect by optimizing the use of resources

   B. Planning can be used to identify potential problems and minimize the chances of making a bad decision

   C. Planning involves understanding the present in order to confront the future

   D. Planning for organizational reasons

4. About the human resource planning process benefits, the author of this passage might disagree that _____ .

   A. it can challenge assumptions

   B. it can minimize the chances of making a bad decision

   C. it can liberate thinking

   D. it can ensuring that long-term thinking is not driven out by short-term focus

5. From this passage, we can infer that _____ .

   A. we should forecast future human resource requirements as a basis for planning and action

   B. there is no evidence that human resource planning works

   C. there is no use for human resource planning

   D. there is no organizational reasons for human resource planning

EIGHT

The criteria or criterion that management chooses to evaluate, when appraising employee performance, will have a major influence on what employees do. The three most popular sets of criteria are individual task outcomes, behaviors, and traits.

If ends count, rather than means, then management should evaluate an employee's task outcomes. Using task outcomes, a plant manager could be judged on criteria such as quantity produced, scrap generated, and cost per unit of production. Similarly, a salesperson could be assessed on overall sales volume in his or her territory, dollar increase in sales, and number of new accounts established.

In many cases, it's difficult to identify specific outcomes that can be directly attributable to an employee's actions. This is particularly true of personnel in staff positions and individuals whose work assignments are intrinsically part of a group effort. In the latter case, the group's performance may be readily evaluated, but the contribution of each group member may be difficult or impossible to identify clearly. In such instances, it is not unusual for management to evaluate the employee's behavior. Using the previous examples, behaviors of a plant manager that could be used for performance evaluation purpose might include promptness in submitting his or her monthly reports or the leadership style that the manager exhibits. Pertinent salesperson behaviors could be average number of contact calls made per day or sick days used per year.

The weakest set of criteria, yet one that is still widely used by organizations, is individual traits. We say they are weaker than either task outcomes or behaviors because they are farthest removed from the actual performance of the job itself. Traits such as having "a good attitude", showing "confidence", being "intelligent" or "friendly", "looking busy", or possessing "a wealth of experience" may or may not be highly correlated with positive task outcomes, but only the naive would ignore the reality that such traits are frequently used in organizations as criteria for assessing an employee's level of performance.

1. According to the passage, which of the following is not the criteria that management chooses to evaluate employees' performance? _____ .

  A. Individual task outcomes   B. Individual behaviors
  C. Individual skills   D. Individual traits

2. Criteria of task outcomes which can be used for a plant manager include the following except _____ .

  A. quantity produced   B. dollar increase in sales
  C. scrap generated   D. cost per unit of production

3. Behaviors of salesperson that could be used for performance evaluation purpose might include _____ .

  A. promptness in submitting his or her monthly reports

B. the leadership style that the manager exhibits

C. number of new accounts established

D. average number of contact calls made per day

4. Traits that could be used for performance evaluation purpose might include the following except _____ .

A. having "a good apperance"

B. showing "confidence"

C. being "intelligent" or "friendly"

D. possessing "a wealth of experience"

5. The author of this passage might most likely agree that _____ .

A. the criteria or criterion that management evaluate employees' performance will have a minor influence on what employees do

B. if means count, rather than ends, then management should evaluate an employee's task outcomes

C. the contribution of individuals whose work assignments are intrinsically part of a group effort can be easy to identify clearly

D. individual traits is the weakest set of criteria that can be used for performance evaluation

NINE

Human resource planning, in the broader meaning of the term, is one of the fundamental strategic roles of the HR function. HR can make a major contribution to developing the resource capability of the firm and therefore its strategic capability by systematically reviewing the firm's strategic objectives and by ensuring that plans are made, which will ensure that the human resources are available to meet those objectives. Thus HR is focusing on the acquisition and development of the human capital required by the organization.

To make this contribution, heads of HR and their colleagues in the HR function need to:

(1) Ensure that they are aware of the strategic plans of the business and can provide advice on the human resource implications of those plans.

(2) Point out to management the strengths and weakenesses of the human resources of the organization, and the opportunities and treats they present, so that these can be considered when developing business plans.

(3) Be capable of scenario planning in the sense that they can identify future issues concerning the acquisition, retention and employment of people and advise on methods of

addressing those issues.

(4) Understand the extent to which quantitative assessments of the future demand for and supply of people may be feasible and useful, and know the methods that can be used to prepare such forecasts.

(5) Understand how to analyze the cost of labor turnover and to establish reasons for leaving.

(6) Be aware of the scope to deal with future requirements by introducing various forms of flexibility.

(7) Be capable of preparing relevant and practical resourcing plans and strategies for retaining people, based upon an understanding of the internal and external environment of the organization and the implications of analyses of labor turnover.

1. In the broader meaning of the term, human resource planning plays a (an) _____ role in the HR function.

　　A. strategic　　B. tactical　　C. objective　　D. critical

2. Which of the following measures isn't the one by which HR can make a major contribution to developing the resource capability of the firm and its strategic capability? _____.

　　A. By systematically examining the firm's strategic objectives

　　B. By ensuring that plans will ensure the available human resources to meet the firm's strategic objectives

　　C. By focusing on the acquisition and development of the people required by the organization

　　D. By focusing on firing and outplacing the redundant employees

3. To make a major contribution to developing the resource capability of the firm and its strategic capability, staff of HR need to do the following except _____.

　　A. ensure that they learn the strategic plans of the business

　　B. point out to management the advantages and disadvantages of the human resources of the organization

　　C. be aware of the scope to deal with existing requirements by introducing various forms of flexibility

　　D. be capable of preparing relevant and practical resourcing plans and strategies for retaining people

4. From the passage, we can't infer that _____.

　　A. human resource planning is one of the HR function

　　B. HR can make a major contribution to developing the resource capability of the

firm and therefore its strategic capability without HR planning
- C. it is the task of all staff of HR to develop the resource capability of the firm and therefore its strategic capability
- D. to develop the resource capability of the firm and therefore its strategic capability, HR must be focus on the acquisition and development of the human capital required by the organization

5. The main topic of this passage is _____ .
   - A. The Contribution of HR to Human Resource Planning
   - B. The Contribution of Human Resource Planning to HR
   - C. The Contribution of HR
   - D. The Contribution of Human Resource Planning

TEN

Job rotation aims to broaden experience by moving people from job to job or department to department. It can be an inefficient and frustrating method of acquiring additional knowledge and skills unless it is carefully planned and controlled. What has sometimes been referred to as the "Cook's tour" method of moving trainees (usually management trainees) from department to department has incurred much justified criticism because of the time wasted by trainees in departments where no one knew what to do with them or cared.

It may be better to use the term "planned sequence of experience" rather than "job rotation" to emphasize that the experience should be programmed to satisfy a training specification for acquiring knowledge and skills in different departments and occupations. It can be argued in support of job rotation that if it is by experience that adults learn, then that experience should be planned.

Success in using this method depends on designing a program that sets down what the trainee is expected to learn in each department or job in which he or she gains experience. There must also be a suitable person available to see that the trainee is given the right experience or opportunity to learn, and arrangements must be made to check progress. For apprentices this will mean the use of training supervisors within departments to see that the training syllabus is followed, and the use of logbooks to record what experience has been gained. The syllabus within a department should include specific assignments or projects. A good way of stimulating trainees to find out for themselves is to provide them with a list of questions to answer; it is essential however, to follow up each segment of experience to check what has been learned, and if necessary, modify the program.

1. What is the main aim of job rotation? _____ .
   A. Acquire basic knowledge   B. Broaden experience
   C. Acquire basic skills   D. Move people from job to job

2. If employers want to broaden employees' experience through job rotation, they must _____ .
   A. plan and control job rotation
   B. move people from department to department
   C. move people from job to job
   D. plan and control the recruitment of employees

3. If we want to make success in using job rotation, we should do the following things except _____ .
   A. design a program that sets down what the trainee is expected to learn in each department or job
   B. ensure a suitable person available to see that the trainee is given the right experience or opportunity to learn
   C. make arrangements to check progress
   D. provide the trainee with no question to answer

4. From this passage, we can't conclude that _____ .
   A. job rotation has never incurred any criticism
   B. the aim of using the term "planned sequence of experience" is to emphasize that the experience should be programmed to satisfy a training specification
   C. if it is by experience that adults learn, then that experience should be planned
   D. a good way of stimulating trainees to find out for themselves is to provide them with a list of questions to answer

5. This passage might be extracted from the paper about _____ .
   A. HR planning techniques   B. selecting techniques
   C. training techniques   D. motivating techniques

ELEVEN

The labor turnover index (sometimes referred to as employee or labor wastage index) is the traditional formula for measuring wastage. It has been described by the CIPD as the "crude wastage method". It is calculated as follows:

$$\frac{\text{number of leavers in a specified period (usually 1 year)}}{\text{average number of employees during the same period}} \times 100$$

This method is commonly used because it is easy to calculate and to understand. For human resource planning purposes, it is a simple matter to work out that if a company wanted to increase its workforce by 50 people from 150 to 200, but the labor turnover rate is 20 percent (a loss of 30 people), then if this trend continues, the company would have to recruit 90 employees during the following year in order to increase and to hold the workforce at 200 in that year (50 extra employees, plus 40 to replace the 20 percent wastage of the average 200 employees employed). It can also be used to make comparisons with other organizations that will typically adopt this method.

This wastage formula may be simple to use but it can be misleading. The main objection to the measurement of turnover in terms of the proportion of those who leave in given period is that the figure may be inflated by the high turnover of a relatively small proportion of the workforce, especially in times of heavy recruitment. Thus, a company employing 150 people might have had an annual wastage rate of 20 percent, meaning that 30 jobs had become vacant during the year. But this could have been spread throughout the company, covering all occupations and long—as well as short—service employees. Alternatively, it could have been restricted to a small sector of the workforce—only 20 jobs might have been affected although each of these had to be filled 10 times during the year. These are totally different situations, and unless they are understood, inaccurate forecasts would be made of future requirements and inappropriate actions would be taken to deal with the problem. The turnover index is also suspect if the average number of employees upon which the percentage is based is unrepresentative of recent trends because of considerable increases or decreases during the period in the numbers employed.

1. The aim of the labor turnover index is to _____ .

 A. measure labor turnover

 B. analyze the reasons of labor turnover

 C. measure costs of labor turnover

 D. analyze the significance of labor turnover

2. If a company has 500 people and its labor turnover rate is 20 percent in a specified period, the labor turnover index of the company is _____ .

 A. 0.2   B. 2   C. 20   D. 200

3. If a company want to increase its workforce from 400 to 500 but the labor turnover rate is 10 percent (a loss of 40 people), then if this trend continues, the company has to recruit _____ employees during the following year.

 A. 100   B. 140   C. 150   D. 200

4. Which of the following isn't the reason that the labor turnover index can be misleading? _____ .

A. The figure may be inflated by the high turnover
B. The labor turnover rate of every occupation may be different
C. The average number of employees upon which the percentage is based is unrepresentative of recent trends
D. The labor turnover index is too simple

5. According to the passage, the author might most likely disagree that _____ .
   A. the labor turnover index is an traditional method for measuring labor turnover
   B. the labor turnover index is commonly used because the calculation is accurate
   C. the labor turnover index can be compared with the one of other organizations
   D. the labor turnover index can be criticized

TWELVE

There are three basic types of employment agencies: (1) those operated by federal, state, or local governments; (2) those associated with nonprofit organizations; (3) privately owned agencies.

Public state employment service agencies exist in every state. They are aided and coordinated by the U. S. Department of Labor, which also maintains a nationwide computerized job bank to which all state employment offices are connected. Using the computer-listed job information, an agency interviewer is better able to counsel job applicants concerning available jobs in their local and other geographical areas.

Although public agencies are a major source of blue-collar and white-collar workers, the experience of some employers with these agencies has been mixed. Applicants for unemployment insurance are required to register with these agencies. They must make themselves available for job interviews to collect their unemployment payments. A fraction of these people are not interested in getting back to work, so employers can end up with applicants who have little or no real desire to obtain immediate employment.

Other employment agencies are associated with nonprofit organizations. For example, most professional and technical societies have units that help their members find jobs. Similarly, many public welfare agencies try to place people who are in special categories, such as those who are physically disabled or are war veterans.

Private employment agencies are important sources of clerical, white-collar, and managerial personnel. Such agencies charge fees for each applicant they place. These fees are usually set by state law and are posted in their offices. Whether the employer or the candidate pays the fee is mostly determined by market conditions. However, the trend has been toward "fee-paid jobs" in which the employer pays the fees. The assumption is that the most qualified candidates are presently employed and would not be as willing to switch jobs if they had to pay the fees themselves. Many private agencies now offer temporary help service and provide secretarial, clerical, or semiskilled labor on a short term basis. These agencies can be useful in helping you cope with peak loads and fill in for vacationing employees.

1. The basic types of employment agencies include the following except _____.

    A. employment agencies operated by federal, state, or local governments

    B. employment agencies associated with nonprofit organizations

    C. employment agencies privately owned

    D. employment agencies owned by the U. S. Department of Labor

2. Which of the following statements about public agencies is false? _____.

    A. They exist in every state

    B. They are coordinated by the U. S. Department of Labor

    C. They are a major source of blue-collar and managerial personnel

    D. They are connected by a nationwide computerized job bank

3. About applicants for unemployment insurance, the author might most likely agree that _____.

    A. they must register with all employment agencies

    B. they must make themselves available for job interviews to collect their unemployment payments

    C. none of these people are not interested in getting back to work

    D. employers can't end up with applicants who have little or no real desire to obtain immediate employment

4. According to the passage, which of the following on private employment agencies can't be concluded? _____.

    A. They are important sources of knowledge workers

    B. Fees that they charge for each applicant are usually in line with state law

    C. Market conditions determine who pay the fees

    D. No private agencies will offer temporary help service and provide secretarial, clerical, or semiskilled labor on a short term basis

5. This passage might be extracted from the paper about _____.

    A. recruitment   B. selection
    C. training   D. performance evaluation

THIRTEEN

Many promotable candidates are originally hired through college recruiting. This is therefore an important source of management trainees, as well as of professional and technical employees.

There are two main problems with on-campus recruiting. First, it is relatively expensive and time-consuming for the recruiters. Schedules must be set well in advance, company brochures printed, records of interviews kept, and much recruiting time spent on campus. Second, recruiters themselves are sometimes ineffective, or worse. Some recruiters are unprepared, show little interest in the candidate, and act superior. Many recruiters also don't effectively screen their student candidates. For example, students' physical attractiveness often outweighs other more valid traits and skills. Some recruiters also tend to assign females to "female-type" jobs and males to "male-type" jobs. Such findings underscore the need to train recruiters before sending them to the campus.

You have two goals as a campus recruiter. Your main function is screening, which means determining whether a candidate is worthy of further consideration. Exactly which traits you look for will depend on your specific recruiting needs. Traits to assess include motivation, communication skills, education, appearance, and attitude.

While your main function is to find and screen good candidates, your other aim is to attract them to your firm. A sincere and informal attitude, respect for the applicant as an individual, and prompt follow-up letters can help you to sell the employer to the interviewee.

1. College recruiting is an important source of the following people except _____ .
   A. management trainees   B. management trainers
   C. professional employees   D. technical employees
2. Which of the following isn't the weakness of college recruiting? _____ .
   A. It is relatively expensive   B. It is relatively time-consuming
   C. It is sometimes ineffective   D. Its main function is screening
3. According to the passage, goals of a campus recruiter include the following except _____ .
   A. screening
   B. determining whether a candidate is worthy of further consideration
   C. printing company brochures
   D. attracting candidates to your firm
4. According to the passage, the author might most likely agree that _____ .
   A. college recruiting can find and screen many good candidates
   B. there is no problem with college recruiting
   C. it is unnecessary to train recruiters before college recruiting

D. it isn't the goal of a campus recruiter to sell the employer to the interviewee

5. This passage mainly discussed _____ .

   A. the problems and goals of college recruiting

   B. the problems of college recruiting

   C. the goals of college recruiting

   D. the methods of college recruiting

FOURTEEN

The managerial grid training as developed by Blake and his colleagues consists of a simple diagnostic framework provided to members to aid them in describing one another's behavior.

The basis philosophy of grid training is that the task of the individual manager is to achieve production through people. In achieving this task, the manager has to show concern both for productivity and people.

Blake suggests that managers can be characterized by their location on a two-dimensional grid, the managerial grid—one axis of which is labeled concern for production and the other concern for people. Each axis is a scale with nine points and so the location of a manager on the grid can be specified by two coordinates. The five principal managerial styles as described in Blake's grid are:

(1) Improved management—exertion at minimum offer to get done the work required to maintain membership of the organization.

(2) Task management where a person is high in task efficiency but low in human satisfaction.

(3) Team management—high task achievement from committed people. Production is achieved by the integration of task and human requirements into a unified system.

A grid seminar is used to teach each participant to see his or her managerial style. Trainees are first familiarized with grid language and theory and then work in groups through a series of exercises and case problems that allow each individual to exhibit management style. This behavior then becomes the object of feedback. Trainees acquire skills in the perception of their own and other people's styles of behavior, and the aim is to move them toward the 9, 9 regions of the grid.

Grid training consists of a series of seminars intended to develop the application of the message throughout the organization. In this respect, it is a type of organization development "intervention" designed to increase organizational effectiveness rather than to concentrate on the improvement of individual interactive skills.

The grid has sound theoretical foundations, being based on a number of research studies. It recognizes the importance of developing an appropriate management style to obtain results by the effort an commitment of work groups. It has plenty of fact validity—ex-grid trainees usually speak highly of it—but research studies are only partially conclusive on its overall effectiveness.

1. The basis philosophy of the managerial grid training is that _____.
   A. the task of the individual manager is to achieve people through production
   B. the task of the individual manager is to achieve production through people
   C. the task of the individuals is to achieve production through other people
   D. the task of the individual manager is to achieve production through himself (herself)

2. Which of the following statements on the managerial grid is false? _____.
   A. It is a two-dimensional grid
   B. One axis of it is labeled concern for production and the other concern for people
   C. Each axis is a scale with nine points
   D. The location of a manager on the grid can be specified by two or more coordinates

3. From the passage, we can draw conclusions on managerial styles as described in Blake's grid except _____.
   A. 1, 1 indicates where a person is low in both task efficiency and human satisfaction
   B. 1, 9 indicates where a person is high in task efficiency but low in human satisfaction
   C. 5, 5 where a person is middle in both task efficiency and human satisfaction
   D. 9, 1 indicates where a person is high in task efficiency but low in human satisfaction

4. About a grid seminar, the author would disagree that _____.
   A. a grid seminar is used to teach each participant to see his or her managerial style
   B. trainees are first familiarized with grid language and theory
   C. trainees can't perceive their own style of behavior
   D. the aim is to move trainees toward the 9, 9 regions of the grid

5. This passage may be extracted from the paper which studied _____.
   A. training   B. performance appraisal
   C. compensation   D. HR planning

FIFTEEN

In collective bargaining, an impasse occurs when the parties are not able to move further toward settlement. An impasse usually occurs because one party is demanding more than the other will offer. Sometimes an impasse can be resolved through a third party, a disinterested person such as a mediator or an arbitrator. If the impasse is not resolved in this way, a work stoppage, or strike, may be called by the union to bring pressure to bear on management.

Three types of third-party interventions are used to overcome an impasse: mediation, fact-finding, and arbitration. With mediation a neutral third party tries to assist the principals in reaching agreement. The mediator usually holds meetings with each party to determine where each stands regarding its position, and then this information is used to find common ground for further bargaining. The mediator is always a go-between. As such, he or she communicates assessments of the likelihood of a strike, the possible settlement packages available, and the like. The mediator does not have the authority to fix a position or make a concession.

In certain situations as in a national emergency dispute where the president of the United States determines that it would be a national emergency for a strike to occur, a fact-finder may be appointed. A fact-finder is a neutral party who studies the issues in a dispute and makes a public recommendation of what a reasonable settlement ought to be. For example, presidential emergency fact-finding boards have successfully resolved impasses in certain critical transportation disputes.

Arbitration is the most definitive type of third-party intervention, since the arbitrator often has the power to determine and dictate the settlement terms. Unlike mediation and fact-finding, arbitration can guarantee a solution to an impasse. With binding arbitration, both parties are committed to accepting the arbitrator's award. With non-binding arbitration, they are not. Arbitration may also be voluntary or compulsory (in other words, imposed by a government agency). In the United States, voluntary binding arbitration is the most prevalent.

1. Which of the following statements about an impasse in collective bargaining is false? _____.

  A. An impasse occurs when the parties are not able to reach an agreement

  B. An impasse usually occurs when one party is demanding more than the other will offer

  C. An impasse can be resolved through a mediator or arbitrator

D. If the impasse is not resolved, the union can't bring pressure to bear on management

2. The types of third-party interventions which can be used to overcome an impasse include the following except _____ .

   A. arbitration   B. fact-finding   C. strike   D. mediation

3. From this passage, we can't draw a conclusion on the mediator that _____ .

   A. the mediator tries to assist the principals in reaching agreement

   B. the mediator usually holds meetings with each party to determine where each stands regarding its position

   C. the mediator is always a go-between

   D. the mediator has the authority to fix a position or make a concession

4. According to the passage, we can infer that _____ .

   A. the president of the United States has the right to determine that a national emergency dispute would be a national emergency for a strike to occur

   B. the arbitrator has no right to determine and dictate the settlement terms

   C. mediation and fact-finding can also ensure a solution to an impasse

   D. in the United States, compulsory binding arbitration is the most popular

5. The best title for the passage might be _____ .

   A. Third-party Interventions

   B. Impasse

   C. Impasse and Third-party Interventions

   D. Arbitration and Mediation

SIXTEEN

Many employers today are supplementing their permanent employee base by hiring contingent workers. Also defined as temporary workers, part-time workers, and just-in-time employees, the contingent work force is big and growing and is broadly defined as workers who don't have permanent jobs.

Just how big is the contingent work force? One way to answer that is to note that in 1993, part-time workers (those employed for less than 35 hours per week) numbered 21 million, or about 17% of the U. S. labor force. Slicing the numbers another way, in 1993 there were 1.7 million people working in the temporary help industry (for temporary help firms like Manpower, Inc. and Kelly Services), up from 732 000 in 1985. Temporary jobs represented 20% of all the new jobs created in the United States between 1991 and 1993.

Contingent staffing owes its growing popularity to several factors. Historically, employers have always used "temps" to fill in for the days or weeks that permanent employees were out sick or on vacation. Increasingly, however, a desire for ever-higher productivity probably explains its growing popularity. In general, as one expert puts it, "productivity is measured in terms of output per hour paid for…if employees are paid only when they're working, as contingent workers are, overall productivity increases." Employers also find that by tapping temporary help agencies, they can save the time and expense of personally recruiting and training new workers, as well as the expenses involved in personnel documentation (such as filing payroll taxes and maintaining absence records). As a result, the contingent work force is no longer limited to clerical or maintenance staff: in one recent year almost 100 000 people found temporary work in engineering, science, or management support occupations, for instance. In fact, growing numbers of firms use temporary workers such as engineers and other professionals to carry out engineering projects, to staff hospitals to meet fluctuating patient loads, and to serve as short-term chief financial officers, for instance.

1. Which of the following isn't contingent workers? _____.

   A. Temporary workers B. Part-time workers
   C. Permanent employees D. Just-in-time employees

2. About the number or percentage of contingent workers in the U.S. in 1993, which of the following is false? _____.

   A. 21 million
   B. 17% of the U.S. labor force
   C. Slicing the numbers another way, there were 1.7 million
   D. 20% of employees who worked for all the new jobs

3. Contingent workers are now growing popular because of the following factors except _____.

   A. employers desire for ever-higher productivity
   B. employers want to fill in for the days or weeks that permanent employees are on vacation
   C. employers can save the time and expense of personally recruiting and training new workers
   D. employers can save the expenses involved in filing payroll taxes and maintaining absence records

4. According to the passage, there are several job areas for contingent workers except _____.

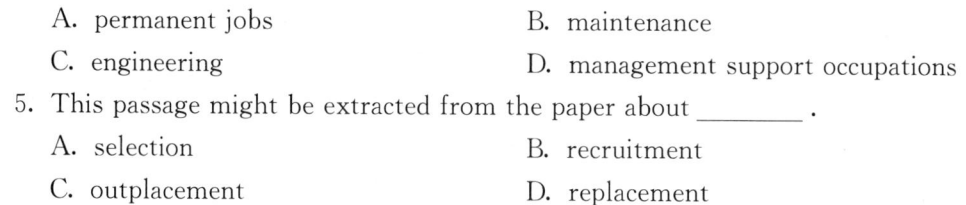

  A. permanent jobs B. maintenance
  C. engineering D. management support occupations

5. This passage might be extracted from the paper about _____ .
  A. selection B. recruitment
  C. outplacement D. replacement

SEVENTEEN

Japanese management gives a great deal of attention to orientation and training, which is particularly true in the case of regular employees. Pre-employment education generally starts immediately after the person is chosen. The purpose of the program is to (1) familiarize the student with the company; (2) monitor the person's activities; (3) make the student comfortable with the company; (4) answer questions the person might have; (5) provide the new employees with any basic skills training the company feels they require.

The appraisal and compensation system is long-term in orientation and is based on rewarding people for doing a good job over an extended period of time. In the United States employees commonly receive an annual appraisal that indicates whether or not they are doing a good job, and if not, provides feedback related to improving performance or seeking employment elsewhere. In Japan the initial appraisal is typically given at the end of a 7-10 years period. At this point the person learns whether or not he or she is going to be promoted up the ranks of management or not. Those who fail this first major evaluation know that their chances of making the top management ranks are virtually nil.

Compensation in Japan used to be based heavily on seniority, but today merit is becoming more important. In many industries the annual raise is in the 2-4 percent range and often is based heavily on merit factors such as attitude, ability, and cooperativeness. Another feature that distinguishes the Japanese system form many others is the semiannual bonus or wage allowance. This bonus is separate from the annual wage increase, and usually without exception, is paid every year regardless of the state of the economy. The bonus is typically equivalent to 5-6 months' salary and is paid in midsummer and at the end of the year. Other forms of compensation include housing allowances, daily living support for transportation, meals, uniforms, health care, and cultural and recreational benefits.

1. The purposes of pre-employment education in Japan don't include _____ .
  A. familiarizing the student with the company
  B. monitor the person's activities
  C. make the student comfortable with the company

D. provide the new hirers with any knowledge and skills

2. The appraisal and compensation system in Japan is based on _____ .

   A. rewarding people for doing a good job over an extended period of time

   B. rewarding people for doing a good job over a year

   C. rewarding people for doing any job over a long time

   D. rewarding people for doing any job over a year

3. In Japan the initial appraisal is typically given at the end of a _____ years period.

   A. 5-10   B. 7-10   C. 10-12   D. 10-15

4. About compensation in Japan, the author would disagree that _____ .

   A. compensation in Japan are based heavily on merit today

   B. merit factors include attitude, ability, and cooperativeness

   C. the main feature that distinguishes the Japanese system from many others is the semiannual bonus or wage allowance

   D. the semiannual bonus equals to 5-6 months' salary

5. From this passage, we can't conclude that _____ .

   A. in Japan, working for a long time in a company is beneficial to employees

   B. the orientation of appraisal and compensation system in Japan is different from the one in the United States

   C. in the United States, employees who commonly receive an annual appraisal can't know whether or not they are doing a good job

   D. employees in Japan may get housing allowances, daily living support for transportation, meals, uniforms, health care, and cultural and recreational benefits

EIGHTEEN

Recruiting is important, because the more applicants you have the more selective you can be in your hiring. If only two candidates apply for two openings, you may have little choice but to hire them. But if 10 or 20 applicants appear, then you can employ techniques like interviews and tests to screen out all but the best.

Some employers use a recruiting yield pyramid to calculate the number of applicants they must generate to hire the required number of new employees. In figure 1, the company knows 50 new entry-level accountants must be hired next year. From experience, the firm also knows that the ratio of offers made to actual new hires is 2 to 1; about half the people to whom offers are made accept. Similarly, the firm knows that the ratio of candidates interviewed to offers made is 3 to 2, while the ratio of candidates invited for interviews to candidates actually interviewed has been 4 to 3. Finally, the firm knows that the ratio of new leads generated to candidates actually invited has been 6 to 1; in other words, of six leads that come in from the firm's advertising college recruiting, and other recruiting efforts, one applicant in six typically is invited to come for an interview. Given these ratios, the firm knows it must generate 1 200 leads to be able to invite 200 viable candidates to its offices for interviews. The firm will then get to interview about 150 of those invited, and from these it will make 100 offers. Of those 100 offers, half (or 50 new CPAs) will be hired.

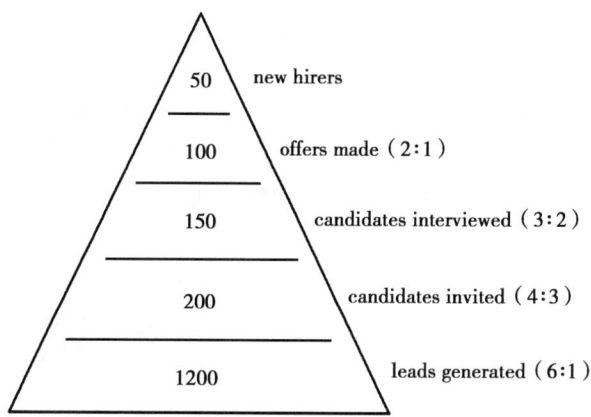

Figure 1 Recruiting Yield Pyramid

The quality of a firm's recruiting process had a big impact on what candidates thought of the firm. For example, when asked after the initial job interview why they thought a particular company might be a good fit, all 41 mentioned the nature of the job; however, 12 also mentioned the impression made by the recruiters themselves and 9 said the comments of friends and acquaintances affected their impressions. Unfortunately, the reverse was also true. When asked why they judged some firms as bad fits, 39 mentioned the nature of the job, but 23 said they'd been turned off by recruiters. For example, some were dressed sloppily; others were "barely literate"; some were rude; and some made offensively sexist comments.

1. A recruiting yield pyramid might include the following except _____ .
    A. offers made   B. candidates rewarded
    C. candidates interviewed   D. leads generated

2. According to the recruiting yield pyramid, if the ratio of new leads generated to candidates actually invited is 5 to 1, the ratio of candidates invited for interviews to candidates actually interviewed is 2 to 1, and the firm want to interview about 100 of those invited, then the firm must generate _____ leads.

A. 200 B. 500 C. 1 000 D. 1 200

3. According to the recruiting yield pyramid, if the ratio of offers made to actual new hires is 3 to 2, the ratio of candidates interviewed to offers made is 5 to 3, and the firm had interviewed 500, then it can hire _____.

A. 50 B. 100 C. 150 D. 200

4. From the passage, we can infer that _____.

    A. if only two candidates apply for two openings, you can employ techniques like interviews and tests

    B. the quality of a firm's recruiting process can influence what candidates thought of the firm

    C. the more applicants you have, the worse your recruitment might become

    D. a recruiting yield pyramid can't be used to calculate the number of applicants they must generate to hire the required number of new employees

5. The best title for this passage might be _____.

    A. Introduction of Recruiting B. Recruiting Yield Pyramid

    C. The Quality of Recruiting Process D. Significance of Recruiting

NINETEEN

Bargaining in good faith is the cornerstone of effective labor management relations. It means that both parties communicate and negotiate. It means that proposals are matched with counterproposals and that both parties make every reasonable effort to arrive at an agreement. It does not mean that either party is compelled to agree to a proposal. Nor does it require that either party make any specific concessions.

When is bargaining not in good faith? As interpreted by the NLRB and the courts, a violation of the requirement for good faith bargaining may include the following:

(1) *Surface bargaining*. This involves merely going through the motions of bargaining without any real intention of completing a formal agreement.

(2) *Concession*. Although no one is required to make a concession, the court's and NLRB's definitions of good faith suggest that a willingness to compromise is an essential ingredient in good faith bargaining.

(3) *Proposals and demands*. The NLRB considers the advancement of proposals as a positive factor in determining overall good faith.

(4) *Dilatory tactics*. The law requires that the parties meet and "confer at reasonable times and intervals". Obviously, refusal to meet at all with the union does not satisfy the positive duty imposed on the employer.

(5) *Imposing conditions*. Attempts to impose conditions that are so onerous or unreasonable as to indicate bad faith will be scrutinized by the board.

(6) *Unilateral changes in conditions*. This is viewed as a strong indication that the employer is not bargaining with the required intent of reaching an agreement.

(7) *Bypassing the representative*. An employer violates its duty to bargain when it refuses to negotiate with the union representative. The duty of management to bargain in good faith involves, at a minimum, recognition that this statutory representative is the one with whom the employer must deal in conducting bargaining negotiations.

(8) *Commission of unfair labor practices during negotiations*. Such practices may reflect poorly upon the good faith of the guilty party.

(9) *Providing information*. Information must be supplied to the union, upon request, to enable it to understand and intelligently discuss the issues raised in bargaining.

(10) *Bargaining items*. Refusal to bargain on a mandatory item (one must bargain over these) or insistence on a permissive item (one may bargain over these) is usually viewed as bad faith bargaining.

1. Bargaining in good faith does not mean that _____ .

    A. both parties communicate and negotiate

    B. proposals are in line with counterproposals

    C. both parties make great effort to reach an agreement

    D. either party must agree to a proposal

2. According to the interpretion of the NLRB and the courts, bargaining may be in good faith when _____ .

    A. both parties have no real intention of completing a formal agreement

    B. both parties are willing to compromise

    C. employers refuse to meet with the union

    D. both parties attempt to impose unreasonable conditions

3. Which of the following isn't a positive factor in determining overall good faith? _____ .

    A. A willingness to compromise   B. The advancement of proposals

    C. Unilateral changes in conditions   D. Providing information

4. From this passage, we can conclude that _____ .

    A. it isn't mandatory to meet and "confer at reasonable times and intervals" for both parties

    B. employers can refuse to negotiate with the union representative in order to bargain in good faith

C. commission of unfair labor practices during negotiations may reflect little good faith of the guilty party

D. insistence on a permissive item can bring bargaining in good faith

5. The best title for the passage might be _____?

A. What is and when is not Bargaining in Good Faith

B. What is Bargaining in Good Faith

C. When is not Bargaining in Good Faith

D. How to Bargain in Good Faith

TWENTY

Fewer 18 to 25-year-olds are entering the work force; this has caused many employers to look into "harnessing America's gray power". Is it practical in terms of productivity to keep older workers on? The answer seems unequivocably to be "yes". Age-related changes in physical ability, cognitive performance, and personality have little effect on worker's output except in the most physically demanding tasks. Similarly, creative and intellectual achievements do not decline with age and absenteeism drops as age increases. Older workers also usually display more company loyalty than youthful workers, tend to be more satisfied with their jobs and supervision, and can be trained or retrained as effectively as anyone.

Recruiting and attracting older workers generally requires a comprehensive HR retiree effort before the recruiting begins. The aim is to make the company an attractive place in which the older worker can work. Specifically:

(1) *Examine your personnel policies*. Check to make sure policies and procedures do not discourage recruitment of seniors or encourage valuable older people to leave.

(2) *Develop flexible work options*. These include part-time, shorter-than-30-hour workweeks, consulting or seasonal work, reduced hours with reduced pay, and flextime.

(3) *Create or redesign suitable jobs*. At Xerox, unionized hourly workers over 55 with 15 years of service and those over 50 with 20 years of service can bid on jobs at lower stress and lower pay levels if they so desire.

(4) *Offer or redesign suitable jobs*. Allowing employees to pick and choose among benefit options can be attractive to older as well as younger employees.

As one expert puts it, to recruit older workers, the message must be tailored to their way of thinking. Appealing to job qualities they value will attract attention. These include flexible hours, flexible benefits, autonomy, opportunity to meet new friends, and working with people their own age. You might also stress that you value their maturity and experience.

1. Which of the age-related changes will affect worker's output except in the most physically demanding tasks? _____ .

  A. Physical ability   B. Cognitive performance

  C. Personality   D. Company loyalty

2. "Harnessing America's gray power", means that _____ .

  A. keeping older workers on

  B. recruiting 18 to 25-year-olds

  C. attracting minorities

  D. encouraging women to enter the work force

3. In order to make the company an attractive place in which the older worker can work, HR staff should do the following except _____ .

  A. examine the personnel policies   B. develop flexible work options

  C. reward at lower pay levels   D. offer or redesign suitable jobs

4. According to the passage, which of the following isn't a flexible work option? _____ .

  A. Shorter-than-30-hour workweeks   B. Full-time

  C. Seasonal work   D. Reduced hours with reduced pay

5. From this passage, we can infer that _____ .

  A. in America, there is no deficit of work force

  B. absenteeism is positively related to ages

  C. flexible work options can be attractive to older workers

  D. to recruit older workers, the message needn't be in accordance with their way of thinking

三、参考答案

(一) 英汉互译

1. 缺席 2. 可接受性 3. 成就测试 4. 行动计划 5. 负面影响 6. 津贴，补助 7. 公告 8. 求职者 9. 申请 10. 评价，评估 11. 平衡计分卡 12. 谈判僵局 13. 行为模拟 14. 行为改变计划 15. 基准 16. 申请求职者，候选人 17. 职业锚 18. 职业咨询 19. 职业曲线 20. 职业发展 21. 职业生涯规划 22. 认知能力 23. 承诺，义务 24. 沟通技巧 25. 报酬要素 26. 报酬，补偿 27. 能力评估 28. 能力模型 29. 竞争优势 30. 妥协 31. 集中战略 32. 商量，请教 33. 持续学习 34. 数据流程图 35. 分散化 36. 决策 37. 缺乏 38. 扁平化 39. 需求预测 40. 沮丧 41. 开发规划系统 42. 差额计件工资 43. 直接薪酬 44. 直接成本 45. 解雇 46. 所得，收入 47. 效率工资理论 48. 效率 49. 平等主义 50. 员工授权 51. 员工租借 52. 雇员调查与研究 53. 企业家 54. 公平就业机会 55. 离职面谈 56. 外派雇员 57. 当面讨论 58. 因素比较法 59. 弹性计划 60. 弹性工作制 61. 流程图 62. 收益分享计划 63. 目标和时间表 64. 群体指导计划 65. 猎头 66. 健康安全 67. 高绩效工作系统 68. 小时工资率 69. 计时工资制 70. 人力资本 71. 收入，收益 72. 间接成本 73. 间接薪酬 74. 通货膨胀 75. 投入 76. 保险 77. 知识资产 78. 内部分析 79. 内部成长战略 80. 内部劳动力 81. 工作分析 82. 工作分类法 83. 工作描述 84. 工作设计 85. 工作扩大化 86. 工作丰富化 87. 工作评价 88. 工作重要性排序法 89. 关键机制，主要机制 90. 劳动关系进程 91. 劳动力流失，人工周转率 92. 无领导小组讨论法 93. 学习型组织 94. 经理评估 95. 目标管理 96. 管理多元化 97. 管理预测 98. 物质奖励 99. 调解 100. 夜班 101. 职业 102. 网上培训 103. 在职培训 104. 实践的机会 105. 组织设计与发展 106. 组织分析 107. 组织结构图 108. 组织代码 109. 小组面试 110. 加薪要求 111. 工资等级 112. 工资结构 113. 按绩效的报酬标准 114. 工资政策线 115. 工资名单，工资总额 116. 养老金，退休金 117. 同事评估 118. 绩效评价 119. 绩效反馈 120. 绩效管理 121. 绩效规划与评价系统 122. 任职要求 123. 人员甄选 124. 计件工资 125. 调查问卷 126. 培训准备 127. 推理能力 128. 和解 129. 认可，承认 130. 人才招聘 131. 冗余 132. 流程再造 133. 拒绝，否决 134. 复职 135. 关联数据库 136. 信度 137. 报酬 138. 声誉，名声 139. 病假 140. 自我评估 141. 社会保险 142. 转包合同 143. 才能，才干 144. 情境面试 145. 技能工资制 146. 技能量表 147. 选拔程序 148. 即时奖金 149. 人员配置表 150. 战略选择 151. 战略一致性 152. 隐性知识 153. 任务分析 154. 团队建设 155. 全面质量管理 156. 工会 157. 培训管理 158. 效用 159. 效度 160. 语言理解能力 161. 既得利益 162. 薪资调查 163. 福利体系 164. 宽带薪酬

165. appoint 166. arbitration 167. assessment center 168. assessment criteria
169. audiovisual instruction 170. audit approach 171. benefit 172. bonus
173. business planning 174. coordination training 175. core competencies
176. cost structure 177. critical incident method 178. cross-cultural preparation
179. cross-training 180. cultural environment 181. cultural shock
182. customer appraisal 183. disparate treatment 184. diversity training
185. dividends 186. discrimination 187. downsizing 188. downward move
189. expert system 190. explicit knowledge 191. external growth strategy
192. external labor market 193. employer of choice plan 194. formal education program
195. frame of reference 196. functional job analysis，FJA 197. group order ranking
198. human resource information system 199. human resource management
200. human resource planning，HRP 201. holistic 202. integration
203. internship programs 204. interview 205. industrialization 206. intrinsic reward
207. job rotation 208. job satisfaction 209. job specification 210. job structure
211. knowledge-based pay 212. line manager 213. lockout 214. merit guideline
215. minimum wage 216. maintenance of membership 217. motivation to learn
218. nonprofit organization 219. orientation 220. outplacement 221. outsourcing
222. overpay 223. power distance 224. position analysis questionnaire，PAQ
225. potential asset 226. project supervisor 227. predictive validation 228. profit sharing
229. promotion 230. psychological contract 231. retention plan 232. repatriation
233. replacement chart 234. return on investment，ROI 235. role analysis technique
236. role play 237. role reversal 238. substantive reason 239. successor
240. supply forecasting 241. strategic human resource management
242. strategy implementation 243. subordinate 244. succession planning
245. training outcomes 246. transnational 247. trend analysis 248. turnover
249. voicing 250. work permit

（二）选词填空

ONE	1. D	2. B	3. I	4. H	5. A	6. J	7. F	8. C	9. E	10. G
TWO	1. H	2. A	3. D	4. C	5. F	6. B	7. J	8. G	9. E	10. I
THREE	1. F	2. C	3. J	4. E	5. A	6. H	7. B	8. D	9. I	10. G
FOUR	1. G	2. J	3. C	4. H	5. A	6. D	7. E	8. B	9. F	10. I
FIVE	1. C	2. G	3. B	4. I	5. F	6. E	7. A	8. D	9. J	10. H
SIX	1. C	2. E	3. I	4. G	5. J	6. B	7. F	8. D	9. A	10. H
SEVEN	1. H	2. E	3. C	4. A	5. F	6. B	7. D	8. I	9. G	10. J
EIGHT	1. E	2. C	3. G	4. J	5. B	6. F	7. A	8. H	9. D	10. I

NINE　　　1. D　2. H　3. F　4. B　5. G　6. J　7. A　8. E　9. I　10. C
TEN　　　1. C　2. G　3. I　4. D　5. B　6. F　7. A　8. H　9. E　10. J

(三) 单项选择题

1. B　2. D　3. C　4. A　5. B　6. B　7. A　8. A　9. B　10. C　11. C　12. D　13. C
14. B　15. B　16. C　17. C　18. D　19. C　20. B　21. B　22. A　23. A　24. A　25. B
26. D　27. D　28. C　29. C　30. C　31. A　32. C　33. C　34. B　35. D　36. B　37. D
38. B　39. B　40. D　41. C　42. C　43. B　44. B　45. D　46. D　47. D　48. B　49. D
50. C　51. A　52. D　53. C　54. B　55. A　56. C　57. C　58. B　59. A　60. C　61. D
62. A　63. B　64. B　65. D　66. D　67. B　68. A　69. C　70. D　71. B　72. B　73. C
74. C　75. C　76. C　77. B　78. C　79. A　80. C　81. B　82. B　83. B　84. B　85. C
86. D　87. C　88. C　89. D　90. D　91. C　92. C　93. C　94. D　95. C　96. C　97. A
98. A　99. B　100. D

(四) 阅读理解

ONE　　　　1. C　2. B　3. D　4. A　5. C
TWO　　　　1. D　2. B　3. A　4. B　5. C
THREE　　　1. B　2. C　3. D　4. B　5. A
FOUR　　　 1. C　2. A　3. D　4. C　5. B
FIVE　　　　1. D　2. B　3. C　4. A　5. B
SIX　　　　 1. D　2. B　3. C　4. B　5. A
SEVEN　　　1. D　2. C　3. A　4. B　5. A
EIGHT　　　1. C　2. B　3. D　4. A　5. D
NINE　　　 1. A　2. D　3. C　4. B　5. A
TEN　　　　1. B　2. A　3. D　4. A　5. C
ELEVEN　　 1. A　2. C　3. C　4. D　5. B
TWELVE　　 1. D　2. C　3. B　4. D　5. A
THIRTEEN　 1. B　2. D　3. C　4. A　5. A
FOURTEEN　 1. B　2. C　3. B　4. C　5. A
FIFTEEN　　1. D　2. C　3. D　4. A　5. C
SIXTEEN　　1. C　2. D　3. B　4. A　5. B
SEVENTEEN　1. D　2. A　3. B　4. C　5. C
EIGHTEEN　 1. B　2. C　3. D　4. B　5. A
NINETEEN　 1. D　2. B　3. C　4. C　5. A
TWENTY　　 1. D　2. A　3. C　4. B　5. C

企业人力资源管理师（三级）鉴定方案

一、鉴定方式

企业人力资源管理师（三级）的鉴定采用机考、笔试方式进行。考核分为 3 个模块，均实行百分制，成绩皆达 60 分及以上者为合格。不合格者可按规定分模块补考。

二、考核方案

考核模块表

职业（工种）名称		企业人力资源管理师		等级		三级	
职业代码							
序号	模块名称	单元编号	单元内容	考核方式	选考方法	考核时间（min）	配分（分）
1	专业知识	1	专业知识	机考	必考	90	100
2	专业技能	1	项目策划	笔试	必考	90	60
		2	案例分析				40
3	专业英语	1	英汉互译	笔试	必考	90	100
		2	选词填空				
		3	单项选择题				
		4	阅读理解				
合　计						270	300
备注							

理论知识考试模拟试卷

一、**判断题**（下列判断正确的请打"√"，错误的请打"×"。每题0.5分，共40分）

1. 人力资源规划的实质是促进企业实现其目标，具有战略性、前瞻性和及时性的特点。（   ）
2. 通过对员工类别分析，可了解一个企业业务的重心所在。（   ）
3. 人力资源信息的审核中，如果发现计算错误导致数据偏差，要采取修正方法，通过对原始数据的再次计算进行更改。（   ）
4. 人力资源需求预测是指根据企业的发展规划和企业的内外条件，选择适当的预测技术，对人力资源需求的数量、质量和结构进行预测。（   ）
5. 人力资源需求预测的方法中，定量预测方法的使用使管理部门直接参与到人才需求预测过程中，综合考虑技术变化、工作负荷变化、组织变化等；而定性方法提供了一种有效的补充信息。（   ）
6. 员工档案是预测人员供给的有效工具，它包含每个人员技能、能力、知识和经验方面的信息。（   ）
7. 以任务为中心的管理哲学把员工视为社会人。（   ）
8. 企业的人力资源管理体系是企业精神、经营理念、价值观念等意识形态的集中表现。（   ）
9. 以任务为中心的管理哲学使用单一的物质刺激作为员工管理和激励的手段。（   ）
10. 工作设计对于激发员工的积极性、增强员工的满意度和提高工作绩效都有重大影响。（   ）
11. 保证工作的深度能使员工有成就感。（   ）
12. 基于团队的岗位设置应用范围不广，可在那些"项目型"的公司中应用。（   ）
13. 工作分析指收集所有与职务相关的信息，以科学和系统的方法确定某职务的性质、职责、任务和要求，决定一项工作所应包含的工作项目及从事此项工作的必备知识、技术和能力，并提供与职务本身要求相关的其他信息。（   ）
14. 工作说明书的编制是对工作分析的结果加以整合从而形成具有企业规章效力的正式文本的过程。（   ）
15. 招聘计划是组织根据部门的发展要求，根据人力资源规划的人力净需求、工作说明的具体要求，对招聘的岗位、人员数量、时间限制等因素做出的详细计划。（   ）
16. 内部招募是指组织采用职位公告、岗位竞聘、部门推荐等方式在组织内部招聘新

员工。（　）

17. 在招聘中录用能力超出职位要求很高的优秀人才，可以为组织储备人才。（　）

18. 知识测验最明显的特点，就是以书面试卷或者口头表述的形式对应聘者提问，有效地测试应聘者在基础知识、专业知识、管理知识、相关知识、综合分析、文字表达等方面的情况。（　）

19. 心理测验的客观性就是指测验能够客观地反映被测试者的心理状况。（　）

20. 一般能力测验，也是通常所说的智力测验。（　）

21. 结构化面试中，面试的内容在面试之前已经形成一个固定的框架（或问题清单），主面试官根据框架对每个应聘者分别进行相同的提问。（　）

22. 录用决策体现择优录用原则，就是广揽人才、选贤任能，在甄选结果的基础上为各个岗位选择最优秀的工作人员。（　）

23. 组织的人才储备通常分为内储和外储两种，内储就是暂时把预留人才储存在组织内部。（　）

24. 新员工培训的目的在于将新录用人员由社会人转变为组织人。（　）

25. 3年以上固定期限和无固定期限的劳动合同，试用期不得超过6个月。（　）

26. 人员配置过程包括招募、选拔和雇用这几个关键的要素，同时还包含了人员流动过程中发生的步骤和活动。（　）

27. 委任制是用人单位通过契约或合同形式聘任干部和员工的一种任用制度。（　）

28. 员工离职的原因包括个人原因、组织内部原因和组织外部原因。（　）

29. 企业要求具备的理想状态与现实状态之间的差距，就是培训需求。（　）

30. 企业的发展过程是一个动态的、不断变化的过程，当组织发生变革时，培训计划也要满足这种变化，是培训需求分析的前瞻性分析的要求。（　）

31. 在任务分析中，任务重要性是对员工完成这些任务的能力要求，这在一定程度上反映了从事此项任务的门槛高度。（　）

32. 只有对组织的使命有较深刻的理解，才能在培训需求分析时做到有针对性和目标性。（　）

33. 在设计培训计划时，要充分考虑人力资源开发的需要，为人才储备打好基础。（　）

34. 培训需求分析主要由两部分工作组成：需求调查和调查实施。（　）

35. 培训需求调查既可以由企业高层管理者、培训主管等发起，也可以通过部门自行申报等形式来收集需求信息。（　）

36. 培训需求分析是整个培训有效进行的前提，也是制订培训开发计划的基础。（　）

37. 培训目标的内容要素包括知识的传授、技能的培养等。（　）

38. 培训计划必须满足组织及员工两方面的需求，兼顾组织资源条件及员工素质基

础，并充分考虑人才培养的超前性及培训结果的不确定性。（   ）

39. 对于长期培训计划而言，时间过长则对有些变数无法做出预测，时间过短就失去了长期培训计划的意义。（   ）

40. 中期培训计划起到了承上启下的作用，是长期培训计划的进一步细化，同时又为短期培训计划提供了参照物。（   ）

41. 为了减少预算时间，应由培训部门独立完成预算编制任务。（   ）

42. 除了直接成本，学员们来参加培训而耽误工作所花费的机会成本也不可忽视。（   ）

43. 预先确定企业内人均培训经费预算额，再乘以在职人员数量的培训预算决定方法，叫费用总额法。（   ）

44. 在每个预算年度开始时，将所有还在进行的管理活动都看作重新开始，即以零为基础，根据组织目标重新审查每项活动对实现组织目标的意义和效果，并在成本收益分析基础上，重新排出各项管理活动的优先次序，是需求预算法。（   ）

45. 比较外部培训和内部培训，企业内部培训是企业培训的发展方向。（   ）

46. 绩效计划最终落实为订立正式书面协议即绩效计划和评估表，它是双方在明晰责、权、利的基础上签订的一个内部协议。（   ）

47. 员工个人信息的准备工作主要包括员工所在岗位的工作描述和员工个人的绩效表现（上一年度的绩效表现及评估结果）。（   ）

48. 绩效计划沟通是计划实施的必要准备工作，不可或缺。（   ）

49. 绩效目标应该来源于企业战略，从企业的最高层开始层层分解绩效目标。（   ）

50. 绩效评估可以定期进行，也可以不定期进行。（   ）

51. 绩效反馈就是评估者将评估结果告知被评估者。（   ）

52. 绩效反馈实施不当，势必引起员工的不满，员工甚至会猜忌评估结果是否被人调整过。（   ）

53. 绩效反馈的重要目的之一是就下一个评估周期的目标进行协商。（   ）

54. 绩效评估结果应有利于人力资源的管理和决策。（   ）

55. 绩效结果反馈给员工，有利于制订绩效改进计划。（   ）

56. 绩效评估结果的应用包括提供有针对性的培训。（   ）

57. 正向激励策略与负向激励策略是改进工作绩效的策略。（   ）

58. 通过绩效面谈，确认工作绩效的不足和差距，查明产生的原因，制订并实施有针对性的改进计划和策略，即为绩效改进计划。（   ）

59. 岗位评价又称职位评估或工作评价，是按照一定的客观衡量标准，采用一定的方法，对岗位的性质、难易程度、劳动强度、责任大小、任职资格等标准进行评价的过程。（   ）

60. 岗位评价的目的是衡量企业内部每一岗位的价值，并建立各岗位价值间的相对关

系。岗位评价的主要依据是工作分析的信息。（   ）

61. 岗位评价主要用于设计薪酬结构和评价任职员工的绩效。（   ）

62. 通过岗位评价，明确了岗位之间的相对价值大小，从而可以为岗位分级分等。（   ）

63. 岗位稀缺性、集体工资协议等都是制约薪酬水平的因素。（   ）

64. 《工资集体协商试行办法》主要是对企业的约束。（   ）

65. 针对不同的部门、不同的岗位、不同的人才，采用不同的薪酬策略，叫差异化薪酬策略。（   ）

66. 工资指数化的目的是降低物价波动对员工工资的影响。（   ）

67. 一岗多薪制下，员工薪酬等级的晋升不以岗位晋升为前提。（   ）

68. 职等是指将不同职系中，工作难易繁简程度、工作责任大小、上岗资格条件等相同相似的职级，纳入统一档次，使各个职级之间打破职系的界限产生纵向的平衡关系。（   ）

69. 宽带薪酬的实质就是从原来注重岗位薪酬转变为注重绩效薪酬。（   ）

70. 做好任职资格及薪酬评级工作，可以缓解宽带薪酬给薪酬成本带来的压力。（   ）

71. 汽车制造业是高科技企业，适合宽带薪酬。（   ）

72. 员工关系指员工与公司、员工与员工之间的关系，就是劳资关系的一个称谓。（   ）

73. 员工关系强调以员工为主体和出发点的企业内部关系，注重个体层次上的关系和交流，关注的是和谐与合作。（   ）

74. 和谐的员工关系是激励员工、减轻工作压力的重要手段之一。（   ）

75. 签订的集体合同要按规定报送地方劳动行政部门审查，以保证集体合同的有效性。生效的集体合同要报上级工会部门备案。（   ）

76. 集体合同是指全体员工与用人单位或者其团体根据法律、法规、规章的规定，就劳动报酬、工作时间、休息休假、劳动安全卫生、职业培训、保险福利等事项，通过集体协商签订的书面协议。（   ）

77. 集体合同的目的是以全体劳动者的共同利益为中心，明确劳动条件和就业条件，如在劳动报酬、工作时间、福利津贴等方面设定具体标准。（   ）

78. 工会成员不足25人的，不可以单独建立基层工会委员会，而需由几个单位联合组建基层工会委员会。（   ）

79. 当基层工会所在的企业关闭、合并、破产、以其他形式终止，或者所在的机关、事业单位被撤销时，基层工会组织可以撤销。（   ）

80. 工会经费的来源主要是工会会员缴纳的会费。（   ）

二、**单项选择题**（下列每题的选项中，只有1个是正确的，请将其代号填在括号中。每题0.5分，共40分）

1. 人力资源信息的准确性、及时性和（　　）决定了它的应用价值。
   A. 有效性　　　　　B. 可衡量性　　　　C. 完整性　　　　D. 可比性
2. 对人力资源信息的审核又称为复查，一般采用（　　）方式进行。
   A. 专家评估　　　　B. 抽样　　　　　　C. 对比　　　　　D. 规划小组讨论
3. （　　）不是影响人力资源需求的外部因素。
   A. 劳动力市场的变化　　　　　　　　B. 政府相关政策变化
   C. 行业发展状况变化　　　　　　　　D. 企业目标的变化
4. （　　）不是影响人力资源需求的内部因素。
   A. 企业目标的变化　　　　　　　　　B. 行业发展状况变化
   C. 组织形式的变化　　　　　　　　　D. 企业最高领导层的理念
5. 相对而言，下面几种人力资源需求预测方法中，（　　）最为简单。
   A. 工作负荷预测法　　　　　　　　　B. 德尔菲法
   C. 现状规划法　　　　　　　　　　　D. 分合性预测法
6. （　　）是适用于较小的项目范围的工作设计方法。
   A. 组织分析法　　　　　　　　　　　B. 关键使命法
   C. 标杆对照法　　　　　　　　　　　D. 流程优化法
7. 制订工作分析的计划、审核和检查工作流程，是（　　）的职责。
   A. 人力资源部　　　　　　　　　　　B. 直线经理
   C. 公司高层领导　　　　　　　　　　D. 外部的专家和顾问
8. （　　）不是任职者在工作分析中的职责。
   A. 参加数据收集　　　　　　　　　　B. 参与工作分析面谈
   C. 参与工作说明书草案的制定　　　　D. 参与工作分析计划的制订
9. （　　）不是人力资源部在工作分析中的职责。
   A. 制订工作分析的计划　　　　　　　B. 对直线经理和任职者进行培训
   C. 提供工作分析专业知识　　　　　　D. 为执行工作分析的多方面工作授权
10. 工作描述的核心内容是任何一份职位描述都必须包含的部分，这些内容一旦缺失，就会导致人们无法对本工作与其他工作加以区分，包括工作标志、工作关系、工作职责、（　　）等。
    A. 工作概要　　　　　　　　　　　　B. 工作权限
    C. 工作环境与工作条件　　　　　　　D. 工作负荷
11. 人力资源信息非常丰富，（　　）不属于常用的人力资源信息。
    A. 人力资源数量　　B. 员工类别　　　　C. 员工素质　　　D. 家庭背景
12. 由于各个企业的自身情况千差万别，在各种因素影响下，获取的人力资源信息就可能出现空白、偏差和失真。（　　）不是常用的补救措施。

　　A. 取舍　　　　　B. 补遗　　　　　C. 复原　　　　　D. 重做

13. 技能档案含有每个人员技能、能力、知识和经验方面的信息，（　　）不是这些信息的常用来源。

　　A. 工作分析　　　　　　　　　　B. 绩效评估

　　C. 教育和培训记录　　　　　　　D. 背景调查

14. 现代企业人力资源管理是以组织中的人为对象的管理，（　　）不是现代人力资源管理的基本职能。

　　A. 录用　　　　　B. 保持　　　　　C. 发展　　　　　D. 竞争

15. （　　）不是岗位设置的主要形式。

　　A. 基于能力的岗位设置　　　　　B. 基于任务的岗位设置

　　C. 基于团队的岗位设置　　　　　D. 基于战略的岗位设置

16. 工作分析小组的成员不包括（　　）。

　　A. 人力资源部人员　　　　　　　B. 工作分析人员

　　C. 外部的专家和顾问　　　　　　D. 工会代表

17. 招聘调研分析主要调研两方面的内容，第一是根据本组织的发展与运行现状，明确工作任务及完成这些任务所需或所缺人员的情况，第二是（　　）。

　　A. 分析本组织整体人力资源或者局部人力资源状况

　　B. 分析本组织人力资源规划及当前的工作任务情况

　　C. 确定招聘的范围、数量、规模等情况

　　D. 确定如何开展招聘工作

18. 如果待招聘人员在人员预算范围外，需要（　　）对招聘的必要性进行审核和论证。

　　A. 人力资源部经理　　　　　　　B. 部门经理

　　C. 公司高层管理人员　　　　　　D. 用人部门

19. 一些调查结果显示，高达90%的管理职位都是由（　　）获得的。

　　A. 外部招聘　　　B. 内部招聘　　　C. 猎头招聘　　　D. 内部竞聘

20. 内部招募的信息覆盖面应是（　　）。

　　A. 有关部门员工　　　　　　　　B. 整个组织内部的全体员工

　　C. 后备人选库中的员工　　　　　D. 公司和部门领导推荐的人员

21. 无论是选拔优秀的员工到更高的职位上工作，还是通过考试将员工安排到更适合他的岗位上去，都应当让广大员工认识到，不断地提高自己的工作能力将会在组织内获得更大的发展空间，这体现了内部招聘的（　　）原则。

　　A. 机会均等　　　　　　　　　　B. 任人唯贤，唯才是用

　　C. 合理配置，用人所长　　　　　D. 激励

22. 在结构化面试中，面试官的人数必须在（　　）人以上。
    A. 2　　　　　　B. 3　　　　　　C. 4　　　　　　D. 5

23. 培训面试官是为了改变传统面试中面试官凭经验和直觉评价的问题，提高面试的准确性。面试培训一般包括了理论知识和（　　）两大部分。
    A. 业务知识　　　B. 实践技巧　　　C. 公司文化　　　D. 职业素养

24. 管理人员等关键岗位，一般由（　　）批准后录取。
    A. 部门经理　　　　　　　　　　　B. 人力资源部经理
    C. 总经理　　　　　　　　　　　　D. 人力资源部招聘经理

25. 在通知被录用者时，最重要的原则是（　　）。
    A. 合法　　　　　B. 及时　　　　　C. 有效　　　　　D. 全面

26. 离职面谈一般由（　　）进行。
    A. 人力资源部　　B. 部门主管　　　C. 公司总经理　　D. 团队负责人

27. （　　）不是外部招聘的主要方式。
    A. 网络招聘　　　　　　　　　　　B. 猎头招聘
    C. 人才市场招聘　　　　　　　　　D. 上级单位任命

28. （　　）不是心理测验对员工招聘的意义。
    A. 提高组织人才甄选的效度
    B. 提高招聘效率，实现批量测评
    C. 可以有效地避免主观性问题
    D. 检查员工是否撒谎

29. （　　）是结构化面试的主要缺点。
    A. 不能减少面试官评价的主观性
    B. 不能控制面试的时间
    C. 不能有效进行应聘者的比较
    D. 不能根据应聘者的不同特点提出针对性的问题

30. 通知应聘者是录用工作的一个重要部分，通知包括录用通知和（　　）。
    A. 聘任协议　　　B. 报到通知　　　C. 离职程序　　　D. 辞谢通知

31. 培训需求分析的基本目标是（　　）。
    A. 确认培训内容　　　　　　　　　B. 确认差距
    C. 确认需培训对象　　　　　　　　D. 确认培训课程

32. 厘清工作绩效不令人满意的原因，是知识、技术、能力的欠缺，还是个人动机或工作设计方面的问题，是（　　）分析要解决的问题。
    A. 组织层面　　　B. 战略层面　　　C. 任务层面　　　D. 人员层面

33. 确定重要的任务，以及需要在培训开发中加以强调的知识、技能和行为方式，以帮助员工完成任务，是（　　）分析要解决的问题。

A. 组织层面　　　B. 战略层面　　　C. 任务层面　　　D. 人员层面
34. 对组织、任务和人员三个层面进行分析时，首先要对（　　）进行分析。
    A. 组织层面　　　B. 任务层面　　　C. 人员层面　　　D. 所有层面一起
35. 任务分析是在特定工作岗位的层次上进行的，主要包括查看工作描述和（　　），确定某项工作的业绩产出标准、要达到此产出标准所必须完成的任务，以及完成这些任务所需的知识、技能、行为、态度等。
    A. 工作规范　　　B. 技术要求　　　C. 任职资格　　　D. 工作关系
36. 当公司进行年末总结和下一年度计划时，应该由（　　）确定培训预算的投放原则和培训方针，以保证培训预算"名正言顺""钱出有因"。
    A. 公司高层领导　　　　　　　　B. 人力资源部经理
    C. 提出培训的部门负责人　　　　D. 第三方机构
37. 如果采用在岗培训的方法，则会出现生产力浪费。专家们估计，在岗培训时所浪费的生产力是正常生产时的（　　）倍。
    A. 1　　　　　　B. 2　　　　　　C. 3　　　　　　D. 4
38. 只有尽可能在预算程序中吸收更多的人，才能更有效地把握公司业务规划和真正的培训需求，从而保证培训预算切实支持公司战略业务发展和员工生涯发展，是（　　）的要求。
    A. 准确性原则　　B. 合作原则　　　C. 速度原则　　　D. 合理原则
39. 培训主管部门要争取和发动从领导到广大员工的参与和有效合作，是（　　）的要求。
    A. 准确性原则　　B. 合作原则　　　C. 速度原则　　　D. 合理原则
40. 承袭上年度的经费，再加上一定比例的变动，是培训预算编制的（　　）。
    A. 比例预算法　　B. 零基预算法　　C. 比较预算法　　D. 费用总额法
41. 培训需求分析是指在需求调查的基础上，由培训主管部门、部门主管和（　　）等采取各种方法与技术，对组织内各部门及其成员的目标绩效与能力结构、现有绩效与能力结构等进行比较分析。
    A. 职工代表　　　B. 公司分管领导　　C. 工会　　　　　D. 员工个人
42. 下面几种培训师中，（　　）培训师是最好的。
    A. 专业型　　　　B. 技巧型　　　　C. 演讲型　　　　D. 卓越型
43. 聘用外部培训师的优势不包括（　　）。
    A. 选择余地大
    B. 带来全新的视角、理念、信息和风格
    C. 提高培训的档次、学员的兴趣和培训的效果
    D. 成本低
44. 在绩效计划的准备阶段，需要准备组织信息、部门信息和（　　）。

A. 经营目标信息　　B. 企业战略信息　　C. 员工个人信息　　D. 考核信息

45. 在绩效计划的准备阶段,组织信息的准备,主要是对（　　）进行重温和再提高、再认识。

　　A. 个人目标　　B. 团队目标　　C. 组织目标　　D. 部门目标

46. 绩效计划的制订必须与组织和部门的总体目标一致,这是制订绩效计划的（　　）。

　　A. 全员参与原则　　　　　　　　B. 可行性原则
　　C. 目标导向原则　　　　　　　　D. 流程系统化原则

47. 在绩效计划审定和确认阶段,直线经理与（　　）必须就绩效计划的主要内容进行再次的讨论和确定,保证双方能就内容所规定的各个方面达成共识。

　　A. 组织高层管理者　　　　　　　B. 人力资源部
　　C. 员工　　　　　　　　　　　　D. 相关部门经理

48. 员工个人绩效目标的来源包括组织的绩效目标、岗位职责和（　　）。

　　A. 内外部客户的需求　　　　　　B. 绩效计划的要求
　　C. 部门的绩效目标　　　　　　　D. 个人职业发展需求

49. （　　）应作为独立的第三方分别与评估人和被评估人面谈,协商并寻求解决纠纷的办法。

　　A. 人力资源部　　B. 主管的上级　　C. 职工代表　　D. 公司分管领导

50. 接受绩效申诉后,查证工作应在（　　）完成。

　　A. 1周内　　B. 2周内　　C. 3周内　　D. 1个月内

51. 绩效评估结果的应用与（　　）紧密结合。

　　A. 员工利益　　B. 主管绩效　　C. 部门利益　　D. 公司利益

52. 绩效评估结果为组织提供总体人力资源质量优劣程度的确切情况,获得所有人员晋升和发展潜力的数据,服务于组织的（　　）。

　　A. 考核制度　　　　　　　　　　B. 培训制度
　　C. 人力资源规划　　　　　　　　D. 招聘和配置计划

53. （　　）不是绩效改进过程中分析工作绩效差距的方法。

　　A. 水平比较法　　B. 目标比较法　　C. 横向比较法　　D. 纵向比较法

54. 一般多用于部门内岗位评估的方法是（　　）。

　　A. 排序法　　B. 分类套级法　　C. 要素比较法　　D. 要素计点法

55. 排序法一般不适用于岗位数量超过（　　）个的情况。

　　A. 10　　B. 15　　C. 20　　D. 25

56. （　　）属于量化的岗位评估方法。

　　A. 排序法　　B. 分类套级法　　C. 要素比较法　　D. 回归法

57. 要素比较法需要选择（　　）个关键岗位。

A. 10　　　　　　B. 10～15　　　　C. 15～20　　　　D. 25
58. (　　) 在岗位评价实践中不太运用。
　　A. 排序法　　　B. 分类套级法　　C. 要素比较法　　D. 要素计点法
59. (　　) 不是绩效管理的主要内容。
　　A. 绩效计划　　B. 绩效实施　　　C. 绩效改进　　　D. 绩效认知
60. (　　) 不是目标管理实施的步骤。
　　A. 工作绩效评估　　　　　　　　B. 提供反馈
　　C. 讨论部门目标　　　　　　　　D. 召开工会动员大会
61. 360度评估法的适用人群为 (　　)。
　　A. 所有员工　　B. 高管人员　　　C. 技术人员　　　D. 营销人员
62. 绩效面谈前，主管人员准备工作包括收集并准备面谈资料、拟订面谈计划、(　　) 等。
　　A. 布置面谈场地　　　　　　　　B. 通知人力资源部面谈计划
　　C. 填写自我评价表　　　　　　　D. 发放面谈通知书
63. 典型的宽带薪酬结构只有 (　　) 个职等。
　　A. 4～8　　　　B. 8～10　　　　 C. 10～15　　　　D. 15～20
64. 传统等级制薪酬的薪酬带宽一般为 (　　)。
　　A. 50%以下　　B. 50%～80%　　C. 80%～100%　　D. 100%～150%
65. 宽带薪酬的薪酬带宽一般为 (　　)。
　　A. 50%～80%　B. 80%～100%　　C. 100%～150%　　D. 不低于200%
66. 对宽带薪酬的描述不正确的是 (　　)。
　　A. 良好的绩效管理是宽带薪酬制度应用的基础
　　B. 技术型、创新型的企业尤为适合宽带薪酬
　　C. 成熟的管理队伍必不可少
　　D. 创业初期企业适合宽带薪酬
67. (　　) 适合采用宽带薪酬。
　　A. 创业期企业　B. 汽车厂　　　　C. 知名外贸企业　D. 银行
68. 要素计点法首先要确定岗位的报酬要素，最常见的报酬要素包括劳动技能、劳动强度、(　　) 等。
　　A. 劳动性质　　B. 劳动工资　　　C. 劳动地点　　　D. 劳动责任
69. 薪酬调查的基准岗位不应该采用 (　　) 的岗位。
　　A. 岗位内容众所周知、相对稳定，且得到从事该岗位员工的广泛认可
　　B. 能代表当前所研究的完整的岗位结构
　　C. 有相当数量的劳动力被雇用
　　D. 具有稀缺性特点

70. 企业可采取的薪酬水平策略主要包括市场领先策略、市场跟随策略、(　　)等。
   A. 弹性薪酬策略	B. 差异化薪酬策略
   C. 随行就市薪酬策略	D. 成本导向策略

71. 员工上岗和离职面谈、人事手续办理、员工申诉和人事纠纷等相关劳动争议处理，属于员工关系管理中的(　　)。
   A. 劳动关系管理	B. 员工纪律管理
   C. 员工人际关系管理	D. 员工绩效管理

72. 组织员工满意度调查、预防及处理员工消极怠工、解决员工关心的问题，属于员工关系管理中的(　　)。
   A. 员工情绪管理	B. 员工纪律管理
   C. 员工人际关系管理	D. 员工绩效管理

73. 不适合作为规章制度的公示方法的是(　　)。
   A. 将劳动规章制度作为劳动合同的组成部分
   B. 将企业劳动规章制度向每位入职员工发放
   C. 以电子邮件和书面公告方式向全体员工公示
   D. 由部门经理向员工进行传达

74. 集体协商双方首席代表可以书面委托本单位以外的专业人员作为本方协商代表。委托人数不得超过本方代表人数的(　　)。
   A. 1/5	B. 1/4	C. 1/3	D. 1/2

75. 生效的集体合同要报(　　)备案。
   A. 地方劳动行政部门	B. 上级工会部门
   C. 工会	D. 董事会

76. 企业、事业单位、机关建立基层工会委员会的条件是工会会员人数在(　　)人以上。
   A. 20	B. 25	C. 30	D. 35

77. 工会经费的来源之一是建立工会组织的企业、事业单位、机关按每月全部职工工资总额的(　　)向工会拨缴的经费。
   A. 2%	B. 3%	C. 4%	D. 5%

78. 基层工会组织可以撤销，撤销时应报告(　　)。
   A. 董事会	B. 劳动行政部门
   C. 上一级工会	D. 职工代表大会

79. (　　)不属于可以撤销基层工会组织的情况。
   A. 所在的企业关闭、合并	B. 所在的企业破产
   C. 所在的机关、事业单位被撤销	D. 工会成员下降到法定数量以下

80. (　　)不是工会的建议权所涉及的范畴。

A. 企业单方面解除职工劳动合同　　B. 劳动安全卫生权利
C. 停工怠工事件　　　　　　　　　D. 员工奖惩处罚

（三）多项选择题（下列每题的选项中，至少有2个是正确的，请将其代号填在括号中。每题1分，共20分）

1. 人力资源信息非常丰富，常用的人力资源信息有（　　）等。
   A. 人力资源数量　　B. 员工类别　　　C. 员工素质
   D. 年龄结构　　　　E. 家庭背景

2. 由于各个企业的自身情况千差万别，在各种因素影响下，获取的人力资源信息就可能出现空白、偏差和失真。在各种补救措施中，修正、（　　）等技术应用得较为普遍。
   A. 取舍　　　　B. 补遗　　　　C. 复原
   D. 判定　　　　E. 重做

3. 技能档案含有每个人员技能、能力、知识和经验方面的信息，这些信息的来源包括（　　）。
   A. 工作分析　　B. 绩效评估　　C. 员工简历
   D. 教育和培训记录　　E. 背景调查

4. 现代企业人力资源管理是以组织中的人为对象的管理，在某种意义和程度上，它至少具有（　　）等基本职能。
   A. 录用　　　　B. 保持　　　　C. 发展
   D. 调整　　　　E. 竞争

5. 外部招聘的主要方式包括（　　）。
   A. 内部员工举荐　　B. 网络招聘　　C. 猎头招聘
   D. 人才市场招聘　　E. 上级单位任命

6. 心理测验对员工招聘的意义在于（　　）。
   A. 提高组织人才甄选的效度
   B. 降低招聘成本，起到优胜劣汰的作用
   C. 提高招聘效率，实现批量测评
   D. 可以有效地避免主观性问题
   E. 检查员工是否撒谎

7. 特殊能力是从事某种活动所需要的能力，包括（　　）。
   A. 数学能力　　B. 音乐能力　　C. 绘画能力
   D. 思维能力　　E. 判断力

8. 结构化面试的缺点主要包括（　　）。
   A. 不能充分发挥面试官的智慧、知识、经验和能力
   B. 不能给应聘者更大的展示才华的空间
   C. 缺少面试官与应聘者之间充分的双向沟通

D. 不能根据应聘者的不同特点提出针对性的问题

E. 面试官评价应聘者的主观性大

9. 通知应聘者是录用工作的一个重要部分，通知类型包括（　　）。

　　A. 录用通知　　　　B. 辞谢通知　　　　C. 聘任协议

　　D. 报到通知　　　　E. 离职程序通知

10. 培训需求分析是指在需求调查的基础上，由（　　）等采取各种方法与技术，对组织内部各部门及其成员的目标绩效与能力结构、现有绩效与能力结构等进行比较分析。

　　A. 培训主管部门　　B. 部门主管人员　　C. 员工个人

　　D. 公司分管领导　　E. 工会

11. 组织层面的分析包括（　　）等内容。

　　A. 明确组织战略导向　　　　　　B. 了解组织氛围

　　C. 了解组织资源　　　　　　　　D. 分析组织人员结构

　　E. 了解员工满意度

12. 绩效管理的内容包括绩效计划、绩效实施、（　　）等。

　　A. 绩效评估　　　　　　　　　　B. 绩效反馈

　　C. 绩效改进　　　　　　　　　　D. 绩效评估结果的应用

　　E. 绩效认知

13. 绩效计划作为绩效管理的一种有效的工具，在制订过程中必须遵守（　　）等原则。

　　A. 与组织和部门的总体目标一致

　　B. 让员工、管理者和其他相关主体参与到绩效计划的制订过程中

　　C. 流程系统化原则

　　D. 贯彻执行原则

　　E. SMART 原则

14. 影响绩效的主要因素有员工技能、（　　）等。

　　A. 外部环境　　　B. 内部条件　　　C. 激励效应

　　D. 目标设定　　　E. 家庭背景

15. 目标管理实施的步骤包括确定企业目标、确定部门目标、讨论部门目标、（　　）等。

　　A. 部门领导与下属人员共同确定长期的绩效目标

　　B. 部门领导就员工实际工作成绩与他们事前商定的预期目标加以比较

　　C. 定期召开绩效评估会议与下属人员展开讨论

　　D. 部门领导与员工共同推进目标的达成

　　E. 召开工会动员大会

16. 360 度评估法主要用于（　　）等几个方面。

A. 评估被评估者的素质、德行、管理能力等与发展相关的绩效
B. 职业发展，指导对员工的培训、调级、调岗
C. 对中高层管理者进行评估
D. 员工发展潜力评估
E. 工会要求全面公平的评估

17. 绩效面谈前，主管人员的准备工作包括（　　）。
A. 收集并准备面谈资料　　　　B. 拟订面谈计划
C. 制订下一步绩效改进计划　　D. 选择面谈的时机
E. 了解绩效考核的方法

18. 岗位评价的方法包括（　　）。
A. 排序法　　　B. 分类套级法　　　C. 要素比较法
D. 要素计点法　　E. 对标法

19. 薪酬结构设计流程包括（　　）。
A. 确定薪酬最小值、最大值
B. 设计工资职等数目
C. 设计工资职等中位值及确定职等薪酬增长率
D. 设计薪酬幅度、薪级数目及薪级差
E. 听取员工意见

20. 从管理职责来看，员工关系管理主要有（　　）等内容。
A. 劳动关系管理　　　　　　B. 员工纪律管理
C. 员工人际关系管理　　　　D. 员工绩效管理
E. 员工考勤管理

理论知识考试模拟试卷参考答案

一、判断题

1. × 2. √ 3. × 4. √ 5. × 6. × 7. × 8. √ 9. √ 10. √ 11. × 12. √
13. √ 14. √ 15. √ 16. √ 17. × 18. × 19. × 20. √ 21. √ 22. × 23. √
24. √ 25. √ 26. √ 27. × 28. √ 29. √ 30. √ 31. × 32. √ 33. √ 34. ×
35. √ 36. √ 37. √ 38. √ 39. √ 40. √ 41. × 42. √ 43. × 44. × 45. √
46. √ 47. √ 48. √ 49. √ 50. √ 51. √ 52. √ 53. √ 54. √ 55. √ 56. √
57. √ 58. √ 59. √ 60. √ 61. × 62. √ 63. × 64. × 65. × 66. √ 67. √
68. √ 69. √ 70. √ 71. √ 72. × 73. √ 74. √ 75. √ 76. × 77. √ 78. ×
79. √ 80. ×

二、单项选择题

1. C 2. B 3. D 4. B 5. C 6. D 7. A 8. D 9. D 10. A 11. D 12. D 13. D
14. D 15. D 16. D 17. A 18. C 19. B 20. B 21. D 22. A 23. B 24. C 25. D
26. A 27. D 28. D 29. D 30. D 31. B 32. D 33. C 34. A 35. A 36. A 37. D
38. A 39. B 40. A 41. D 42. D 43. D 44. C 45. C 46. C 47. C 48. A 49. A
50. A 51. A 52. C 53. D 54. A 55. B 56. C 57. C 58. C 59. D 60. D 61. B
62. D 63. A 64. A 65. D 66. D 67. C 68. D 69. D 70. D 71. A 72. A 73. D
74. C 75. B 76. B 77. A 78. C 79. D 80. D

三、多项选择题

1. ABCD 2. ABC 3. ABD 4. ABCD 5. BCD 6. ABCD 7. ABC 8. ABCD
9. AB 10. ABC 11. ABC 12. ABCD 13. ABC 14. ABC 15. BCD 16. ABC
17. ABCD 18. ABCD 19. ABCD 20. ABC

专业技能模拟试卷

一、项目策划题一（30分）

案例背景

风华实业发展公司是一家生产制造型企业，经过20多年的努力，公司业务快速发展，在行业中颇具知名度。公司目前共有生产制造与设备维修人员825人，行政和文秘人员143人，中层管理人员79人，设计和产品研发人员38人，销售人员23人。近5年来，员工的离职率为14%，不同类别的员工离职率不一样，其中设计和研发人员离职率较高，达20%以上。

公司为了进一步发展，制定了5年战略发展目标，规划在新的业务领域开发出几种有吸引力的新产品，期望公司5年内销售额翻一番。为了适应公司整体经营发展战略的要求，人力资源部开始着手准备公司的未来5年人力资源规划。

在人力资源规划时首先要进行人力资源需求分析。人力资源部主要听取了各部门负责人的想法。各部门负责人为了使自己部门将来的人手能够充足，纷纷强调自己部门的重要性，提出了很多对人员的要求，包括人数、人员结构、层次等方面。人力资源部基于这些数据汇编出公司未来的人力资源需求表，却发现庞大的人员需求量和高学历人才需求量是公司难以承受的，也无法确定如何才能落实未来的人才措施。

案例思考

1. 该公司在人力资源需求预测中存在什么问题？（14分）
2. 如何进行公司人力资源需求预测？（16分）

二、项目策划题二（30分）

案例背景

2017年1月5日，乔天成去琴谱公司应聘技术主管一职，经过2轮面试后公司告诉他回去等消息。2017年2月10日，琴谱公司对5位候选人面试后，决定录用乔天成。人力资源部经理让招聘专员给乔天成发录用通知，由于招聘专员正忙于筛选另一个职位的应聘者资料，直到2017年2月25日才使用私人邮箱给乔天成发送了录用邮件。

乔天成打开招聘专员发来的邮件，见邮件中写道："你申请的技术主管一职，经公司讨论已同意录用，请你于3月15日前来我公司报到。办完入职手续后，你需要参加我公司为期1个月的培训。如不能按时报到，视作本人放弃。"乔天成不明白到底什么时间报到比较合适，以及报到还有些什么其他要求。于是乔天成通过邮件进行了询问，得到的答复是："上午10:00前。"乔天成还有些不放心，又给琴谱公司发送了一封邮件，希望琴谱公司给他发送一份正式的录用通知书。

案例思考

1. 琴谱公司在录用过程中存在哪些问题？（12分）
2. 请为琴谱公司起草一份新员工录用通知书。（18分）

三、案例分析题一（20分）

案例背景

普华科技发展公司是一家网络销售和服务企业，成立于2012年，拥有100多名员工。由于公司以网络平台作为销售方式，十分注重人际沟通能力和团队合作能力，因此从公司创办初期就对员工的培训十分关注。在企业发展过程中，公司根据业务特点和需求，设置了课程目标及相关课程，聘请了专业讲师，培训确实也对企业的经营发展起到了积极作用。

近几年，公司业务规模在迅速扩大，组织结构发生了一些变化，90后员工人数也在不断增加。但2018年，公司的培训计划基本还是前几年的版本，培训讲师依然是外聘的，培训目标及培训课程也没有变化。但是员工的培训体验却越来越差，培训课程所获得的效果也不令人满意。不少员工反映培训内容与工作实际有较大的差异，与企业现在的业务相关性不大；有些培训内容对90后员工而言过于说教，学习积极性较差；单纯的授课方式比较沉闷，无法调动大家的学习兴趣；有些对管理能力的培训要求全员学习，很多基层员工对管理理论的内容无法理解。公司管理层要求人力资源部查找原因，并提出解决方案，改变目前培训状况。

案例思考

1. 普华科技发展公司的培训计划存在哪些问题？（8分）
2. 该公司应如何改进培训计划？（12分）

四、案例分析题二（20分）

案例背景

福德公司是一家电子设备股份制企业，随着公司业务的不断发展，员工人数不断增加，如何有效管理员工、提升企业绩效成为公司重要的管理议题。2017年起，公司开始注重绩效管理工作，通过一系列培训，使员工们也初步了解了有关绩效考核的具体要求。

韩晓德是研发部的技术人员，入职已有10个月。2017年年底，研发部经理胡建军通知韩晓德要进行绩效考核结果反馈谈话。韩晓德有些不安，因为平时胡经理比较忙，他们之间很少有沟通交流的机会。

在绩效反馈谈话中，胡经理对韩晓德的表现总体是肯定的，除了认为他与领导的沟通不够主动、个性内向、不善表达、工作中有时缺乏与同事主动配合、有效协助不够等，总体还是觉得韩晓德的工作态度是好的。由于胡经理接下来要参加公司战略规划会议，整个谈话只进行了10分钟左右，韩晓德没有机会表达自己的想法，对工作中与同事之间曾产生的误会没有来得及反馈，对一些工作中的困惑和改进方法也未充分交流。

韩晓德在收到的绩效评估书面报告中发现胡经理写了他在工作中的不少问题，而对他

的成绩和优点只稍微描述了几句,有些问题也和实际情况不符合。

案例思考

1. 胡经理在绩效结果反馈时未能遵循哪些原则?(8分)
2. 胡经理该如何改进绩效结果反馈?(12分)

专业技能模拟试卷参考答案

一、项目策划题一（30分）

答题思路

1. 该公司在人力资源需求预测中存在的问题

（1）未能从现实人力资源需求、未来人力资源需求和未来人力资源流失等多角度进行人力资源需求预测。（8分）

（2）未能与公司战略有机结合，人力资源需求分析未能考虑内外部的各类影响因素。（3分）

（3）部门经理提出的人力资源需求存在主观性，缺乏明确的依据，影响预测的客观性。（3分）

2. 进行人力资源需求预测的步骤

（1）进行现实人力资源的需求预测。与相关部门的经理沟通确定现有的职务编制和人员配置，进行现有内部人力资源盘点，统计出各部门的缺编、超编是否符合职务资格要求，讨论确定现实需求人数。（4分）

（2）进行未来人力资源的需求预测。根据公司发展规划和部门业务目标确定工作量。根据工作量增长情况，确定各部门职务编制和人员配置，明确需增加的职务及人数，并进行汇总统计。（4分）

（3）进行未来人力资源流失预测。结合公司退休和各职位离职率等情况，对未来可能的流失人数进行预测。（4分）

（4）将现实人力资源需求预测、未来人力资源需求预测和未来人力资源流失预测进行汇总，即可预测出该公司的人员需求，以此为依据为后续人力资源招聘等一系列人力资源管理工作奠定基础。（4分）

二、项目策划题二（30分）

答题思路

1. 公司在录用过程中存在的问题

（1）公司做出录用决定后未能及时通知应聘者。（4分）

（2）录用通知的内容不完整，具体时间不明确，未写明应聘者需要携带的办理入职手续所需要的资料等信息。（4分）

（3）录用通知形式不正确。（4分）

2. 起草录用通知书

录用通知书（标题 2 分）

乔天成先生：

　　您好！

　　您应聘本公司的技术主管职位，经面试复核审议，决定录用您为本公司员工，欢迎您加盟本公司。请您于 2017 年 3 月 15 日上午 10 时到本公司人力资源部办理入职手续。（8 分）

　　办理入职手续需要提供以下证件和资料。

　　（1）录用通知书。

　　（2）居民身份证原件。

　　（3）毕业证书、学位证书原件，原单位离职证明、与工作相关的资料。

　　（4）体检报告（区、市级以上医院体检证明）。

　　报到后，本公司会组织入职培训，帮助您尽快适应工作环境。如果您有什么疑惑或困难，请与人力资源部联系。电话：021-******。

　　如果您不能按时就职，请于××××年××月××日前告知本公司人力资源部。

琴谱公司人力资源部（公章）

人力资源部经理：×××

2017 年 2 月 25 日（8 分）

三、案例分析题一（20 分）

答题思路

1. 培训计划存在的问题

（1）培训目标不合理。培训目标没有随着公司业务发展和员工需求进行合理调整。（2 分）

（2）培训对象选择不合理。培训内容与学员的工作岗位不匹配。（2 分）

（3）培训内容没有结合培训需求和培训对象进行适当调整。（2 分）

（4）培训形式过于简单。单一的外部讲师授课式培训方式，无法取得较好的培训效果。（2 分）

2. 改进培训计划

（1）培训目标要和组织的目标相吻合，要基于培训需求分析的结果来确定。（3 分）

（2）合理选择培训对象，了解培训对象的学习和岗位内容，有针对性地确定培训对象。（3 分）

（3）培训内容需要进行重新设计，应该结合组织、任务、人员的需求进行优化。（3 分）

（4）培训形式需要与培训内容、培训对象有机结合，选择有针对性的培训方式。（3

分)

四、案例分析题二（20 分）

答题思路

1. 绩效结果反馈时未遵循的原则

（1）未能遵循坚持具体全面原则。胡经理的绩效结果反馈中，定性内容的反馈为主，缺乏对员工存在问题的具体事实的列举。(3 分)

（2）未能遵循坚持互动原则。本次反馈中胡经理只是进行反馈观点的陈述，未留时间给与韩晓德进行交流，引导其自诉。(3 分)

（3）未能遵循坚持正面引导原则。胡经理提出韩晓德不足之处后，未能进一步提出改进思路，未能共同制订绩效改进计划。(2 分)

2. 改进绩效结果反馈的思路

（1）胡经理应该做好绩效结果反馈的准备，包括绩效结果反馈时间的安排、反馈内容的准备（如绩效事实准备、对绩效改进的思考等）。(4 分)

（2）胡经理在绩效结果反馈中，一方面应以事实为依据进行绩效反馈，同时也要引导被反馈者说出自己的想法，实现有效的互动，澄清一些问题。(4 分)

（3）胡经理在绩效结果反馈中要强化对未来绩效改进的引导和辅助，积极帮助被反馈者改进绩效行为，为未来提高绩效制订有针对性的计划。(4 分)

专业英语模拟试卷

一、英汉互译（请将下面的英语译成汉语，汉语译成英语。每题2分，共30分）

1. post
2. self-appraisal
3. minimum wage
4. night shift
5. job enlargement
6. gain sharing plans
7. lockout
8. welfare system
9. markov analysis
10. questionnaire
11. 情境面试
12. 心理契约
13. 任务分析
14. 人力资本
15. 网上培训

二、选词填空（请选择正确的单词，将其代号填在横线处，使句子意思完整。每题2分，共20分）

| A. empowerment | B. workforce | C. integrated business | D. pattern |
| E. audit | F. strategy | G. sign up | H. flexible | I. business |
| J. free agency |

1. In a high-demand world, quality, innovation, _____, customer focus, team building, productivity, and so on, are all necessary.

2. One reason for company's success was its culture, which was based on open communication and an entitled _____ (well-trained, highly committed, knowledgeable workers).

3. The outcome of _____ is an architecture of framework for incorporation HR practices into business decisions to ensure results.

4. New _____ emerge when ideas create new frameworks, new ways of doing

work, and new expectations for the work held by both HR professionals and clients.

5. In retail chains, organizational _____ is considered an essential complement to financial assessment.

6. A firm using the impact and implementability criteria employed the method to turn _____ into action.

7. The automated system allows employees to _____ and change benefits using an interactive voice-response system.

8. The service center mission is "to provide highly accessible and _____ world class human resource services to all employees."

9. Generalizing ideas means sharing knowledge across boundaries of time, space, geography, _____ or function.

10. A business needs to encourage _____ and autonomy in making decisions, sharing information, and soliciting ideas.

三、单项选择题（下列每题的选项中，只有1个是正确的，请将其代号填在横线处。每题2分，共20分）

1. An interview in which an applicant is given a hypothetical incident and is asked how he or she would respond to it is a _____.
   A. computer interview   B. panel interview
   C. situational interview   D. nondirective interview

2. Which training method focuses upon learning at the affective level? _____.
   A. sensitivity training   B. apprenticeship training
   C. intercultural motivation   D. multilingual training

3. The Hay profile method uses which three factors for evaluating jobs? _____.
   A. knowledge, skill, and responsibility
   B. mental ability, skill, and responsibility
   C. knowledge, mental ability, and responsibility
   D. knowledge, mental ability, and accountability

4. The performance evaluation approach which compares each employee with every other employee and rates each as either the superior or the weaker member of the pair is known as _____.
   A. the paired comparison   B. the individual ranking
   C. the group order ranking   D. critical incidents

5. The area from which employers obtain certain types of workers is known as the _____.
   A. labor market   B. region

C. recruiting area   D. supply region

6. The job specification describes job requirements relative to _____.
   A. skill and physical outputs   B. skill and physical demands
   C. age and physical demands   D. experience and physical description

7. The final decision to hire an applicant usually belongs to _____.
   A. the HR recruiter   B. the HR manager
   C. line management   D. co-workers

8. Hiring someone outside the company to perform tasks that could be done internally is known as _____.
   A. outplacement   B. contracting
   C. outsourcing   D. employee leasing

9. The lines of advancement for an individual within an organization are known as _____.
   A. career paths   B. job progressions
   C. career lines   D. job paths

10. The purpose of a profit-sharing plan is to _____.
    A. allow workers to contribute specific knowledge to improving the organization
    B. motivate a total commitment to the organization as a whole
    C. enable workers to share in labor cost savings
    D. instill commitment to the employees' immediate work group

四、阅读理解（阅读以下2篇短文并做短文后面的单项选择题。每题3分，共30分）

ONE

Because of the progress of technology, human resource managers are better also to service the needs of their colleagues and their employer. As Human Resource Manager, the challenges posed to them in the age of advancing technology are great and each manager must utilize the resources available to them in order to perform their functions effectively. HR personnel must constantly keep up to date with change and therefore must experience on going training to keep abreast with development. A wonderful resource is the internet and here at this venue, managers are able to obtain current information on technological changes through web-based training.

In today's society, everything now is computer based. Standard systems have been developed to record and store information. Programs have been designed to analyze inputted information thereby giving the HR professional a wide variety of information. Information is easy to store and easily accesses.

Emailing is now a necessity. Instantaneous communication is possible not only with words but with sound and picture. It is easy to interface with employees, colleagues, and business partners and associates.

It is apparent that technology will continue to grow at a rapid pace. It is the responsibility of the Human Resource Personnel to be aware of these changes and their implication for their department. Training and computer learning are essential if the HR Manager hopes to continue as a professional and contributing worker.

1. According to the passage, who do not the human resource managers service to? _____.

  A. The co-workers   B. The customers

  C. The line manager   D. The senior management

2. What is not the element of the instantaneous communication? _____.

  A. Photo   B. Music   C. Text   D. Smell

3. According to the passage, the author might most likely disagree that _____.

  A. managers can obtain current information on technological changes through web-based training

  B. programs have been designed to analyze inputted information

  C. email is difficult to interface with employees, colleagues, and business partners and associates

  D. training and computer learning are essential if the HR Manager hopes to continue as a professional and contributing worker

4. From this passage, we can't conclude that _____.

  A. standard systems have been developed to record and store information

  B. it is the responsibility of the Human Resource Personnel to be aware of the changes of the technology

  C. each human resource manager must utilize the resources available in order to perform their functions effectively

  D. it is better to arrange regular training for human resource manager regarding the update idea of technology

5. This passage mainly discussed _____.

  A. how does HR deal with technology

  B. the new requirements for HR manager

  C. the technology and HR

  D. the tendency of HRM

TWO

Teams often turn modest individual efforts into extraordinary success. Studies of high performing teams provide clear evidence that teams can often leverage average individual talents into superior collective achievements, when faced with high demands; teams often find better ways to solve demands than do individuals working in isolation.

Boeing provides an example of teamwork in action to meet extraordinary demands. The Boeing 777 air frame, the foundation of Boeing's twentieth-century fleet, was created under exceptionally difficult demands. It had to be completed in less time than previous models had been; it had to be produced at less cost and be fuel efficient beyond any aircraft in the air; it had to meet very high customer performance expectations; and it had to please the pilots who would fly it. These demands did not have clear, or in some cases, even available answer. More than two hundred teams participated in the design, engineering, manufacture, and assembly of the Boeing 777, however, and the results redefined.

Teams are often accused of being slow to come to decisions. Actually, in many cases, the opposite has been true. In situations of high demands, where answer and solutions are readily available, teams used as resources can focus members' attention and more rapidly resolve issues than can individuals. Hallmark has established itself as the standard for greeting cards; as competition grew from American Standard and other brands, however, Hallmark executives knew they would have to rethink how work was accomplished.

6. The purpose of the example of Boeing 777 is _____.

   A. to provide that teamwork plays an important role

   B. to prove that Boeing 777 is an example of teamwork to meet demands

   C. to find out that teams turn modest individual efforts into success

   D. to discover that Boeing 777 could not be succeed without teamwork

7. Which of the following can be inferred from the passage? _____.

   A. Teams usually can do better than individuals

   B. Answer and solutions are readily available

   C. Teams can leverage average individual talents into collective achievements

   D. All the above

8. According to the example of Boeing 777 which of the statements can not be inferred? _____.

   A. It had to be produced at less cost and be fuel efficient beyond any aircraft in the air

   B. It had to be completed in less time than previous models had been

C. It had to meet very low customer performance expectations

D. It had to please the pilots who would fly it

9. Why did not the author agree with teams are often accused of being slow to come to decisions? _____.

A. Teams used as resources can focus members' attention and more rapidly resolve issues than can individuals

B. In many cases, the opposite has been true

C. Teams' efficiency are very high

D. Teams often rethink how work was accomplished

10. The best title for the essay is _____.

A. The challenging work

B. The reason of Boeing's success

C. Collaboration

D. Demands of team

专业英语模拟试卷参考答案

一、英汉互译
1. 职位，岗位
2. 自我评估
3. 最低工资
4. 夜班
5. 工作扩大化
6. 收益分享计划
7. 停工
8. 福利体系
9. 马克夫分析法
10. 调查表，问卷
11. situational interview
12. psychological contract
13. task analysis
14. human capital
15. online training

二、选词填空
1. A 2. B 3. C 4. D 5. E 6. F 7. G 8. H 9. I 10. J

三、单项选择题
1. C 2. A 3. D 4. A 5. A 6. B 7. C 8. C 9. A 10. B

四、阅读理解
1. B 2. D 3. C 4. D 5. A 6. B 7. D 8. C 9. A 10. C